# THE MAGIC OF EMOTIONAL INTELLIGENCE FOR THE ATHLETE & COACH

## THE OPEN SECRET TO BUILDING TEAM CHEMISTRY

JAMES DAVID

# THE MAGIC OF
# EMOTIONAL INTELLIGENCE
# FOR THE ATHLETE & COACH

## THE OPEN SECRET TO
## BUILDING TEAM CHEMISTRY

Printed in the United States of America

Cover art design by Rachel Crockett Preiser

First edition published 2018

# TABLE OF CONTENTS

# FOREWORD

Being a championship player and building a winning team takes more than athletic prowess and skillful coaching. The best players and coaches in the world aren't successful unless their ability to manage their complex emotions in the heat of the competition matches their skill in the game. Sports pages are full of examples of coaches and athletes losing both their cool and the game when their emotions take over.

Today, sports is a global enterprise and athletic teams are noticeably more multicultural, having athletes from all over the world. Along with their skill, players bring their different backgrounds, cultures, and norms to the group. This reality makes building a winning team even more complicated and challenging. For optimum results, both players and coaches need to be in tune with themselves and each other, and also know how to use the power of emotional energy to propel them to success. Understanding and getting along with their diverse teammates is not a luxury; it is essential to achieving successful outcomes.

This book gives players and coaches the critical information and know-how they need to capture and manage the power of emotions to increase their individual and team performance and to manage emotions so they don't sabotage success in the game.

Through powerful stories and concrete, actionable steps to follow, the author gives athletes and coaches a roadmap and guide.

Lee Gardenswartz, Ph.D. and Anita Rowe, Ph.D.

*Knowing others is intelligence.*
*Knowing yourself is true wisdom.*
*Mastering others is strength.*
*Mastering yourself is true power.*

Lao Tzu

# INTRODUCTION

Africa, the world's greatest wilderness. It's the only place on Earth where you can still witness the full majesty of Mother Nature. From lazy lions sleeping under a baobab tree to the mighty elephant swimming across a river, Africa is much more than I could have ever imagined. Ever since I was a kid, it had been a lifelong dream for me to visit and this summer I finally got my chance. Even though I was able to look eye-to-eye with some of this world's most amazing animals, it was a story I heard during a fishing trip that had the most impact on me.

I had decided that the perfect way to end my two-week trip to Africa was to spend a few days fishing on the mighty Zambezi River. I discovered a little place located in the western part of Zambia called the Mutemwa Lodge. It was a fisherman's paradise: plush beds inside big green canvas tents, guided fishing, amazing food, and above all, the hosts Gavin and Penny Johnson are simply one of a kind. After spending some time with the Johnsons, I found out that Gavin was quite a former athlete himself and was on the 1995 South African rugby team that won the World Cup. I equate its significance to the USA men's Olympic 1980 miracle on ice—it's that big of a deal! In fact, it was such a big deal that they made a movie about it starring Matt Damon called *Invictus*.

As cool as it was meeting Gavin, it was a guide named Francis who gave me a life lesson I will never forget.

The Zambezi River is filled with more than just fish. Eighteen-foot crocs and hippos with foot-long incisors that range from 3,000 to 9,500 pounds also call the river home.

Some people think I might be crazy going fishing where there are a lot of crocodiles and hippos lurking in the water, but in reality as long as you are in a bigger boat with a motor and pay attention to your surroundings, they will leave you alone.

But if you're in a canoe, it's a whole different story. We had just passed a pod of hippos huddled together by a small island when I asked our guide if he'd ever had a close call with a hippo. "Oh yes!" Francis replied. And that's when he told me about his close encounter with death.

Francis lives in a village on the opposite side of the river of the fishing lodge. It is about a two-mile walk from the river to his home. After his walk, he gets into his canoe and paddles across the river to the fishing lodge and starts his day guiding.

Since this is rural Africa, most of the homes are made of a red clay-like mud and have thick brown straw roofs. Very few people have electricity (generators) because it is difficult to find a job here. Most villagers live off the land, which includes making your own canoe—called a *makoro*—which takes several weeks to craft.

Francis had gotten off work early and was just about to paddle across the river when a girl from another village asked him for a ride. Like most all of the people who live there, Francis helps anyone he can.

As he reached the middle of the river, he was looking into the sky, noticing how beautiful the day was. What he didn't notice was that a hippo had swum directly beneath his canoe.

*WHAM!* The hippo hit the bottom of the canoe and he and his passenger were thrown into the water. Francis was now in panic mode. His very first thought was *I'm dead.*

Once a hippo tips you over, they will come from underneath and attack with their giant teeth. An attack by a hippo is so violent that it can easily cut a person in half.

Francis looked down into the water; all he saw was the pink back of the hippo run underneath him. By God's grace the hippo didn't attack him and just ran toward open water. But this didn't mean that it wouldn't come back.

In a panicked voice, Francis called out for the lady and found her hanging on the other side of the overturned canoe.

He knew how dangerous the water was— eventually, they would pass over another hippo, or, even worse, a croc. Reality started to sink in. Francis realized he was going to die and never see his family again.

## THE DECISION

Francis' only lifeline was a floating upside-down waterlogged canoe. He had a wife and two young daughters at home, and another person he barely knew floating down the river with him, relying on him for survival.

Should he stay with the canoe and *hope* someone would see him and the girl or should they swim for shore and take a chance on them becoming an easier target for crocs and hippos? That's the situation Francis faced.

What would you do?

Francis knew his time to make a decision was running out every passing second. He decided to ask the lady with him if she could swim to the shore. "Yes," she replied.

He looked upriver; the closest land to him was an island. Then he looked downriver; it was a much longer swim to the shore, but he wouldn't be fighting the current. The island was still the better bet, as it was closer.

As Francis started to swim for it, a few hippos popped up, angrily blowing water from their nostrils and blocked his path.

Downriver became his only choice.

Francis and the girl started swimming downriver and both were becoming more and more exhausted. When he neared the shore, he heard a giant splash.

To him it meant only one thing: a crocodile had just entered the water.

Francis froze in place, silently treading water. This time he knew for sure he was dead. He waited for the giant jaws to lock onto him and pull him under the water—but they never did.

It was just a tiger fish that had jumped out of the water and made that splash. Realizing this, Francis continued to swim toward the shore where he heard the splash.

Just as he was about to get onto land, Francis heard a cry for help. "Francis, please come back, I can't swim any farther!"

As he looked back, he saw the girl's head go underwater.

## THE MORAL DECISION

*She's dead*, he thought.

And then her head popped back up and she continued to yell.

"Please, I can't make it, I'm going to drown. Please come back!" Her head again slipped underwater.

People die all the time when trying to help someone else who is drowning. Most of the time it's because the person drowning is so terrified that they latch on to the person who is trying to save them. They both panic, and typically both die. This was fresh in Francis' mind. *If I go back, we are both going to die. I'm too exhausted to help her. I can't save her*, he thought.

*The shore is RIGHT THERE. I can make it—I can see my wife and kids again. I am not going to die. I should just keep going, there is nothing I can do for her.*

Somehow he was able to push those thoughts of safety aside.

"I will come back, but you have to promise me you will not grab on to me. If you do, we are both dead!" he yelled.

Her face was barely out of the water and she was really struggling now. With what was probably going to be her last breath, she called out, "Okay."

Francis turned around and began to swim back into the deep water, swimming to save her.

When he reached her, he threw his arm around her chest and asked her if she could help him swim back. "No," she said. "I cannot; I am too tired."

"Here, grab on to the back of my belt and hold on tight," he instructed. "Kick your legs as hard as you can and help us swim."

Exhausted, they barely made it back to shore. Both of them collapsed onto the ground, crying. They clung to each other, unable to speak.

Now that they were both going to live, they stood and started their long journey back to the village. When they arrived, he was unable to tell his wife and daughters what happened. It was still too traumatic. All he could do was embrace his family and cry.

## THE CANOE

If you were like me, as I was listening to this story you probably had forgotten about the canoe. In my mind, it was trivial—the furthest thing I cared about. But to Francis, it was his livelihood. He asked two of his friends to give him a lift back to the fishing camp so he could use one of the motorboats to retrieve his canoe. The whole ordeal had left him so shaken that he had to have his friends paddle the canoe while he sat in the middle with his head down. Every time he looked into the water, all he saw was a hippo jumping out of the water at him. I told Francis he probably had HIPPO-PTSD.

As they approached the canoe, they saw that it had also picked up another visitor: a giant crocodile.

"I would have died for sure if I'd stayed with the canoe," he told me. He had made the right decision to leave the canoe.

What did you get from this story?

The first thing I understood was that Francis was prepared. He understood his environment. He knew how hippos and crocodiles interact within their environment.

When he first heard the big splash next to shore, he swam toward the splash where he first thought the crocodile was. Why? Once he figured out it was not a croc and instead a fish, he knew that there were no crocodiles near because fish do not hang around where crocs are.

He was able to keep his emotions in check and did not panic. This gave him the ability to think clearly and make the best decision possible.

Second, he knew that eventually a croc or hippo would be curious about the floating canoe and would want to check it out. He knew he couldn't stay with his only lifeline and made the difficult decision to leave the canoe.

In life, there are many times fear paralyzes us from making the logical decision and we decide to stay with what we are most comfortable with. We are afraid to leave the "canoe"—sometimes even if we know, like Francis did, that it would eventually kill us.

Lastly, Francis *got back in the water* for someone he barely knew. He was truly selfless, able to block out all thoughts of self-preservation and make a decision to save someone's life.

There are people "drowning" around us all the time—people we may know really well or people we don't know at all. I think we all need to take a page from Francis and be ready to go into the water for the people we barely know and be their lifeline.

After the hippo attack, Francis could have easily asked his boss for a ride home every day by motorboat or by land. But he didn't. He knew he had to eventually get back in the water with his canoe and overcome his fear. He still, to this day, doesn't take the easy way out.

The difference between winning and losing a game is a fraction of a second. Throughout this book you'll learn that emotional intelligence (knowing how to interact with people in different environments and understanding how emotions affect every decision in your field of play) is the key to creating and maintaining a healthy team that competes at optimal performance. Like  Francis, you'll learn that you have the ability to make sacrifices for others—and that's what will help you win more games.

Let's get started.

# CHAPTER 1
## *Magic & Sports*

My love for sports started as a kid living in Wisconsin. My mother and father separated when I was six years old. They were both young and I went to live with my grandparents so my mother could get back on her feet. I spent the majority of my time with my grandparents helping out my grandfather, who had been paralyzed a few years earlier from a motorcycle accident. Living his life having to use a wheelchair was especially difficult for him. It not only prevented him from doing the things he used to be able to do, but it also limited his ability to take me places (much less take me outside and teach me a sport). Looking back, I guess that's why we spent a lot of our time watching sports on TV.

Most people view Wisconsin as the state that only has cows and cheese…which is partly true. But something outsiders don't really know about is our extreme passion for sports. My grandfather and I would watch everything from football to baseball to golf. Even though the Green Bay Packers are the king of the state, of all the sports we watched, tennis seemed to be his favorite and it quickly became my favorite too. When I was old enough, he enrolled me in my first tennis lesson. I would pretend to be John

McEnroe as I would try to smash tennis balls across the net like him.

I had lived with my grandparents for about a year when my mother showed up with a guy I had never seen before and whisked me away to a different state. Over the next few years that seemed to be the theme, as we moved many times from state to state before finally settling in Southern California. Because we moved so much, I was forced to make new friends quite frequently and I became pretty good at it.

We moved to a trailer park and made it our home in Castaic, CA. Tennis was not popular here and I soon found out that two-hand touch football in the back alley was the game of choice. A mailbox at the end of a driveway was usually what counted as the end zone. I was younger than most of the kids I played with and their version of touch football usually led to many scraped-up knees and bloody hands, so I had to grow up faster than other boys my age.

It wasn't until we moved again in the seventh grade that my affair with basketball began. Once again, I found myself trying to make friends quickly and I saw some kids playing basketball at lunch. One of the older boys asked me if I wanted to play. I was a little hesitant at first because I didn't know much about the sport, but after being called for double dribble and traveling a bunch of times, I finally got the hang of it. I had one thing going for me though: I was really tall for my age, which helped me overcome my lack of skill in the beginning. I could grab rebound after rebound and shoot until I scored. Once I got better at dribbling, it didn't take long for me to fall in love with the sport. Just like that, basketball was now in my blood.

Back then, like most kids, I was oblivious to the correlation between life and sports. I was just playing for the same reason almost everyone does—to have fun. But looking back after spending many years playing and then coaching basketball, I realized that so many lessons about life *are* taught in sports. I'm sure I'm not telling you something that you haven't heard before. However, it seems that as athletes, we don't *really* get it until we are done playing. Sports and life definitely mirror each other, and just like in sports, life has certain fundamentals as well. How well you use them will determine how successful you become in each. Emotional intelligence is a fundamental principle of life. When you learn and apply it to your life, things tend to get better.

## MAGIC

It was in the middle of my second year as a head basketball coach and I was listening to a speaker at a coaching conference talk about the stress of coaching sports. He said something that changed the direction of my life: "If you ever *really* want to be good at your job, you need to find a hobby that takes your mind off of it. It should be something that you like doing so much it gives you a mental break from your profession."

The next day I was sitting at home watching the film after a tough loss, thinking about all the things we did wrong in that game. The more I watched, the more upset I got. I decided to stop watching and turned on the TV. A new magician had just come out with a special; his name was David Blaine.

I watched David perform miracles with a deck of cards and other ordinary objects to people on the street. It was then that I knew exactly what my next hobby was going to be.

Magic.

But I had a problem. I never played with cards growing up. In fact, I wasn't even good at shuffling. My very first thought was filled with doubt. *There's no way I'll ever be able to do any of those tricks*, I thought. I mean, most magicians typically start at a very young age, but I was already twenty-nine years old.

The following day I searched the Internet and found my first magic video. It was called, "The Foundation of Card Magic."

When the preview was playing I thought it was going to be much too difficult for me to learn. Guys were flipping cards in the air and making entire decks of cards disappear. I was wrong. I soon found out that the very first thing you need to do is learn how to hold the cards.

*Hold the cards?* I thought. It reminded me of something Vince Lombardi, the former head coach of the Green Bay Packers, would say to his players at the beginning of every season. He would start his training camp by saying, "Gentlemen, this is a football."

In magic terms, the basic way to hold the cards is called a "mechanic's grip." Most every card trick is based on this one fundamental.

Once I learned how to hold the cards, I learned the many ways to shuffle them. Next was how to hold a "break," a technique that allows you to keep the deck separated without anyone seeing you do it. These shuffling and break techniques allow you to do different types of "forces," which is when you make people pick the card that you want them to pick. Each subsequent move you learn slowly builds to learning a harder fundamental of magic.

I began to practice for hours at a time, mastering the basics of each technique. I cannot tell you how many times I dropped cards and had to pick them up and start over... I'm sure it was in the thousands.

I would do the same trick over and over again until it looked perfect. The more I practiced, the better I got. And the better I got, the more people began to love watching me perform. My confidence was growing and I noticed that I wasn't nervous anymore.

It wasn't until I was preparing a practice plan one day that I realized magic and sports are identical. They both have fundamentals, and each one leads to performing a more difficult task.

After a show, my former mentor and I were driving through the streets of Boston, discussing what it takes to be a good performer on stage. He said, "James, I am going to tell you a secret about performing magic. You see, anyone can do a trick, but not everyone can do magic. In order to do magic, you have to actually *believe* that you are doing magic."

I understood exactly what he meant. It's the same when I see a fundamentally sound team perform and execute flawlessly. The more you practice the fundamentals, the better you are at executing those skills. When you master them, that's when execution turns from a "trick" into "magic."

Some teams go to practice and put in the bare minimum. Sure, they show up, but they are un-coachable or selfish. They don't want to flawlessly execute the fundamentals because it's "boring." Players might say they want to win, but it's only if they are playing. They do not believe.

The teams that believe in what the coach is telling them tend to believe in mastering the fundamentals, believe in one another, and believe they are the best—and they tend to actually *do* the best. My stage presence became so much better because I knew that I was mastering the fundamentals of my performance, and it showed by my audiences' reactions, which translated into more gigs.

The same holds true for your team, regardless of your sport. Understanding the fundamentals of emotional intelligence will transform your team into a competent group of individuals who understand each other's needs and as a result, perform better.

What's the secret? Emotional intelligence.

# TALKING POINTS

*Q: What are two things that you took away from the opening story? Explain why they impacted you.*

*Q: What do you do to relieve stress in your daily environment?*

(Please use the space below to write your answers)

- How he learned different sports by just moving around for me I learned most of my sports by going to games and meets, plus P.E. class. His hobby now when he lost a game he gained a new hobby. When I just have a lot of free time so I read.

- I don't know what relieves my stress.

# CHAPTER 2
*What is EQ?*

The whistle blows and the fans in the stands scream so loudly that you think your ear drums might explode. Sweat is trickling down your face and your muscles begin to tighten. Your heart beats hard against your chest; you're sure everyone can see it. It all comes down to this: The next point can win it all. How do you handle the pressure?

I used to only think of sports as having two basic parts: physical conditioning and mental conditioning. Now I believe we need to add a third to the list, *emotional conditioning.*

Emotional intelligence (also known as EQ, for emotional quotient) is a term that has been around for quite a while now. It was a term first coined by Peter Salovey and John D. Mayer in 1990.

But famous author Daniel Goleman in his book, *Working with Emotional Intelligence*, seemed to bring it into popularity. But just because it has been around for a while doesn't mean that EQ is a well-known term. Sometimes when the subject comes up, some people say they have heard of it, while others have no clue what I'm talking about. Especially when it comes to relating it to sports.

Emotional intelligence is defined as "the conscious recognition of different emotional states, the ability to assess how one's emotions affect his or her behavior, and the ability to manage emotions and act appropriately based on certain situations."[1]

If you think that emotional intelligence is about "touchy feely" stuff, you're not necessarily wrong. But it's not about everyone holding hands, singing hymns, and living in utopia, either. I believe it lies somewhere in the middle.

I used to think that the smarter a person was, the easier it was to control his or her emotions. But during my research for this book, I have discovered that there is a big difference between IQ and EQ. An individual's IQ—or intelligence quotient—is the number used to describe that individual's relative intelligence. It's the ability to concentrate, learn, interpret and analyze facts. While IQ can develop and increase as they age, once an individual reaches adulthood, IQ test scores remain somewhat constant: the older you are, the more stable your IQ test score will be. Under normal circumstances, studies say that it changes very little, if at all.

EQ, on the other hand, is the ability to understand your emotions and the emotions of others. It's the ability to handle stress, to look at beliefs or opinions that differ from yours and to keep an open mind. Someone with a high EQ is self-aware of his or her emotions and actions. They will always

[1] Goleman, Daniel. "What Is Emotional Intelligence." Institute for Health and Human Potential.
https://www.ihhp.com/meaning-of-emotional-intelligence.

put themselves in other people's shoes and try to understand another's viewpoint. Emotionally intelligent people are not afraid to take criticism and are always looking to expand their knowledge. They also tend to be the kind of people that others like to hang out with—and more importantly, enjoy working with. Many studies suggest that people with a high EQ are four times more successful in their professional field.[2]

As a sports coach, what I discovered about EQ has changed my perception of sports, athletes, people, and life.

This book is written for coaches and athletes alike, in the hopes that both can see how the other benefits from being trained in emotional intelligence. Because athletes and coaches do not have a lot of extra time, I purposely made the book as short as possible without cutting corners.

Although some parts of the book are directed to coaches and others to players, it's important for both coaches and athletes to read the *entire* book to gain perspective of both sides and understand how knowledge of EQ can help increase everyone's effectiveness inside and outside of sports.

I have seen it play out in my life with our kids. I first had this thought when I was extremely frustrated

---

[2] Deutschendorf, Harvey. "Why Emotionally Intelligent People Are More Successful." Fast Company. https://www.fastcompany.com/3047455/why-emotionally-intelligent-people-are-more-successful.

with my toddler over potty training. It was then that I penned this letter to my former high school coach:

*Hey Coach, so I'm sitting at home with my toddler, Tommy, who is by far the most stubborn little boy ever. I am currently in a heated battle with him over potty training. He refuses to give into what I am trying to teach him and I refuse to stop training him. Then it hit me.*

*Coaching a sport is kind of like potty training a toddler. It can be extremely messy and disgusting at first. You have to have a lot of patience and yet still be firm, even when the toddler or the player is stubborn and refuses to learn. But as frustrating as it is, we cannot let them just sit in a stinky diaper forever. There has to be a consequence for not doing the things that we ask—whether it's putting Tommy in a time-out when he has wet underwear, or conditioning and potentially losing playing time for the athlete. However, in both potty training and in sports, it's better in the end when the skills are developed and used properly.*

*If you fail at the fundamentals in either case, YOU STINK!*

## WHY EQ IS IMPORTANT

*"You don't have to control your thoughts. You just have to stop letting them control you."*

*– Dan Millman*

Emotional intelligence in the realm of sports encompasses many genres: self-confidence, compassion, teamwork, leadership, and excellent communication with self and others. To truly succeed in sports, an athlete must associate his or her passion for the sport with enthusiasm and grit. An athlete who is enthusiastic and excited about coming to "work" is statistically more likely to perform better on the field. The more emotionally intelligent an athlete is, the more likely he or she is to know how to act both on the field and in life, and when to get into a specific mindset. On the other hand, an athlete who cannot control his or her emotions on the field, for example, would be considered less successful than the athlete who can act rationally and calmly, especially when it involves teamwork and sportsmanship.

This is because they are better at building relationships, are better teammates, and make better employees when they enter the workforce. When they are done with their playing careers, they climb the ladder of success much faster through promotions, make more money, and have many more valued friendships. Individuals who have high emotional intelligence are more effective at managing their emotions and actions, making them more successful at interpersonal communication. In other words, the emotionally intelligent athlete is more successful when working with others on a team.

# WHY EQ IS IMPORTANT FOR ATHLETES

At the core of it all, EQ is physiologically important for athletes because of biology. When you are faced with a pressure-filled situation, your heart begins to race, the blood from your stomach rushes to your limbs, your body releases adrenaline, and clarity of thought is compromised.[3]

If you are not able to cope with your biological responses to stress, you may not make the best choices when a problem or challenging situation presents itself.

Much like the muscle memory skill of a basketball player when shooting a ball, your brain is like a muscle that can be re-trained and programmed to learn new skills. EQ is no different—the more you practice, the better skills you will have at managing your emotional response to a challenging situation. An emotionally intelligent player can bypass this biological reaction and reclaim control over his or her actions.

I often hear a coach or sports figure say that the "lights are brighter" when it comes to the play-offs. This is not actually true. The lights are not literally brighter, but they *seem* brighter due to the pressure of

---

[3] "How Stress Affects Your Body and Behavior." Mayo Clinic. https://www.mayoclinic.org/healthy-lifestyle/stress-management/in-depth/stress-symptoms/art-20050987.

the moment because the adrenaline causes your senses to be more acute.[4]

Some players or teams cannot control their excitement in these big games. They let their emotions get the better of them and more often than not, the desired goal is not reached. Emotional intelligence will teach a player to get off the rollercoaster of emotions and "dim the lights."

This happened during my senior year when our team first played our cross-town rival in a huge road game. We were picked to finish first in our conference and they were picked to finish second. The atmosphere and energy inside the gym made it feel like a play-off game. We were all really excited to play and you could feel the intensity of it in every person on the team.

But all of that excitement changed to anger and frustration when things didn't go well for us in the beginning of the game. We didn't know how to handle our emotions and made mistakes that were not typical for our team. Some of our players lost their temper and a technical foul was handed out to one of our best leaders. We tried to regroup at halftime but even a fiery speech from our coach couldn't save us, and in the end, we were blown out. It wasn't because we didn't have a good game plan or were not prepared skill-wise. It was because we couldn't control our emotions.

---

[4] Ibid.

After the coaching staff had some time to reflect, the next day at practice our assistant coach told us that looking back, we had the most intense warm-up he had ever seen before a game. We were overhyped and we let our excitement and emotions control us.

*We lost because we couldn't dim the lights!*

## WHY EQ IS IMPORTANT TO SPORTS

Why does this relate to sports? Because it has been around for so long, I believe emotional intelligence is the open secret to building team chemistry in your program.

But how do you apply it? In order to find the solution to a problem, sometimes you have to work the problem backward. Let's work it out and start at the end—winning a championship.

What does it take to win a championship?

The first and obvious thing you need is **some talent**. I'm not saying you have to be the most talented team, but you definitely can't be talent-less. Then you need to have **strong team chemistry**, which includes a passion for the sport and a passion to get better. Athletes must push each other on *and* off the court, and they must share a common bond or common goal.

You need **strong leadership** and **you have to be coachable**. You must have players who **build strong relationships with each other.** You must recruit players who **believe in**, **respect**, and **trust** one another—this last one is especially important. In *any* relationship, from romantic to business, if you do not have trust, that relationship will not live up to its potential or will eventually fail.

In order to build trust with someone, **you have to be likable** in your actions. That's not to say you always have to be liked, but you can't be a total jerk all the time. But here's the million-dollar question: How do you teach a person how to be likable? Is it even possible?

I think everyone has the capability to be likable—they simply must be *willing to learn* and apply the four quadrants of emotional intelligence:

1. **Self-Awareness**: *To be self-aware means you must really understand your personality: your strengths and your weaknesses.* In other words, what do you say or do sometimes that can annoy others around you. I call them personality "blind spots." I liken it to someone having "coffee breath," I know it but they don't. You are also aware of what motivates you and what does not.

2. **Self-Management:** *The ability to regulate your emotions.* You don't get too high or too low when stressful situations arise. You don't allow your emotions to rule your thoughts and actions. You know when to use your

emotions at the right time and in the correct way.

3. **Social Awareness:** *The biggest part of this is being empathetic.* You have the ability to put yourself in other people's shoes and genuinely care about the other person. You understand that people are raised with different sets of morals and values. Some may come from different socio-economic backgrounds and even broken or abusive homes.

4. **Relationship Management:** *You not only understand yourself, but you also understand other people's personalities.* Understanding this gives you the ability to adapt and relate to people who differ from you. It makes you more likable.

If you learn and study emotional intelligence, ask yourself the tough questions and apply these concepts to your life. By doing so, you will become more emotionally intelligent—you will become more likable. Being more likable will give you the ability to build stronger relationships and to gain trust. Like a domino effect, once you gain trust, you start to build team chemistry.

Since you can teach and learn emotional intelligence, you can teach and learn how to foster team chemistry, allowing you to maximize your talent, which correlates to maximizing your chances to win championships. See how everything flows together?

## TALKING POINTS

*Q: What is EQ?*

*Q: Which quadrant of EQ is your strongest and which one is weakest in your personality?*

*Q: What can you do to strengthen your weakest quadrant?*

- Emotional intelligence

- I think my strong suit is that I'm realistic to others and can be fun to be around my weak spot is that I'm quiet

- try talking more

# CHAPTER 3
*Self-Awareness*

*"Being self-aware is not the absence of mistakes, but the ability to learn and correct them."*

*— Daniel Chidiac*

Hope Solo was the goalkeeper for the USA national women's soccer team—and by all standards, one of the greatest goalkeepers in the world, having appeared in 202 international games and winning more than 75 percent of them.[5] But that changed when she hurled insults at Sweden after their team lost in the 2016 Rio Olympics.

After the Swedish team chose to take a conservative approach to the game, causing the US team to become frustrated and ultimately lose the highly favored game, she called them "a bunch of cowards"—and was kicked off the team for unsportsmanlike behavior.[6]

It might seem over the top for her to get kicked off the team for a statement that could be seen as just being that of a "sore loser," but unfortunately most of her career has been plagued by controversy. Even

---

[5] Mahler, Johnathan. "Hope Solo's Behavior, and Play, Spells End With U.S. Team." *The New York Times*. Retrieved from https://www.nytimes.com/2016/08/26/sports/soccer/hope-solo-us-womens-team-terminated-contract.html
[6] Ibid.

before the 2016 Olympics, she drew criticism by tweeting a picture of herself in a beekeeper's mask with cans of bug spray spread out on her bed in reference to the Zika virus. While some might see this as a lighthearted joke, to the Brazilians it was an insult.

Her lack of self-awareness and the inability to control her emotions led her to make numerous mistakes and plagued the USA Soccer Federation with controversy because of her actions. The sad part of this is that these were self-inflicted wounds—and her Olympic career was cut short because of her lack of self-awareness.

Hope Solo excelled at stopping a soccer ball from entering the goal, but the one thing she couldn't stop…was herself. Her lack of basic consideration of others' feelings ultimately led to her dismissal from the team.

## DEVELOPING SELF-AWARENESS

Having self-awareness is the foundation to personal growth and success. Self-awareness is all about being able to recognize and understand how our interactions are affected by our emotions, and how our emotions impact the emotional state of others. To keep our emotions in control we need to realize that we are in control of our emotions. We are the boss here. During his address to the Governing Board of the Pan American Union in April 1939, U.S.

President Franklin D. Roosevelt famously said that "Men aren't prisoners of fate, but only prisoners of their own minds. They have within themselves the power to become free at any moment." These were powerful words coming from a person who knew a thing or two about making decisions under pressure and how not to let emotions take control of the decisions.

It's no surprise that Roosevelt's insight is shared by many thought leaders, because it highlights the opportunity for us to achieve the ultimate freedom. The key to better decisions, greater confidence, and assertiveness is the ability to stop reacting to events and learn how to choose your response according to the situation. But first, we need to learn more about ourselves. This is where self-awareness comes in.

The good news is, awareness of yourself and your emotions can be developed. Here, let's focus on the ability to recognize your emotions and use them for the better of yourself and others.

**Keep a Journal**
When you feel emotionally stressed, write down what had occurred and why you reacted in a particular way. Was there any physical reaction, such as, a sore neck, headache, or racing heart etc.?

**Make a List of Your Roles**
Make a list of all of the roles that you play in your life, or the roles you identify yourself with, and how they

affect you. These should include both the roles you were born into and the roles you have adopted. The idea is to find your identity and who you are in relation to the roles you play in life. You may be a mother, sister, daughter, father, brother, employee, husband or wife, and even a sportsman or woman. Try to think of as many roles as you can and jot down your feelings for each role you are playing in your life. They might be, happy, afraid, anxious, etc.

## Predict Your Feelings

This might be a bit harder to do, but you can get better by trying. First, think of a situation that you may experience, then predict the way you would feel during that situation. Practice naming those situations and the corresponding feelings for each situation, such as fear, anger, sadness, joy, surprise, disgust, etc. By naming the emotional states, you will be able to put yourself and your emotions in control. When you are faced with any situation, try to choose an appropriate feeling rather than just reacting to it without thinking. For example, some of the most uncomfortable situations often involve dealing with a teammate or a coworker—the people who we interact with on a daily basis, and are maybe borderline friends with. Whenever a problem arises, it is important to deal with the situation delicately. If you have to deal with a problematic coworker, try having a discrete conversation with the person rather than blowing the war horns. As you learn to develop your self-awareness, your own interpretations and thoughts will begin to change.

Another way you can build self-awareness is by setting some time aside daily for meditation and self-reflection. Using meditation techniques can help you open your mind to deeper thoughts, and possibly become more self-aware in the process.

## Value & Beliefs

Our values are the morals, principles, and ideals that help guide us through life. Knowing our values is a critical part of building self-awareness. It's like driving down a highway that has many signs posted so you always know where you're going. You are comfortable and secure since you know exactly where you are headed, and you're confident knowing that your path will eventually take you toward your destination. That's how values and beliefs work in the journey of life.

## Assumptions

Another important aspect of developing emotional intelligence is developing an awareness of the assumptions we have about others, or the assumptions we hold about ourselves. These can be both positive and negative. Take some time to think about a task you performed at the office, or a tactic you used at a game. Now, what were your immediate thoughts about your ability to complete the said task, or perform during a game? Regardless of your thoughts being negative or positive, it is important to spend some time to think about how these thoughts make you feel. Do they help or hinder the completion of a task? And how can you turn a thought around the next time? Try writing those thoughts down. If they are negative thoughts, think of a more preferred positive thought to replace the negative thoughts. Do the same for the thoughts you have while thinking about others; how those thoughts make you feel and how you can change these negative thoughts (assuming they are negative) into positive ones. The thoughts or beliefs we have about ourselves and others are important since they determine our mental and physical behavior.

Since self-awareness is the foundation of emotional intelligence, we should take the time to learn more about ourselves. As we improve our self-awareness, and our ability to respond to change, we will improve our experiences in life, create new opportunities and improve our game.

# TALKING POINTS

*Q: Think about a time that you might not have been self-aware. How would you handle it differently?*

*Q: What are a couple of your personality "blind spots"?*
*(Hint: If you can't think of any, you are NOT self-aware! My suggestion is to ask someone you already trust and keenly listen to their critiques.)*

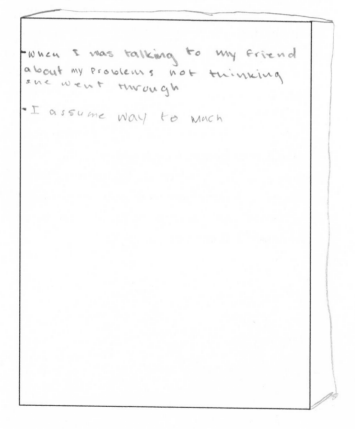

- When I was talking to my friend about my Problems not thinking she went through

- I assume way to much

# CHAPTER 4
## *Self-Management & The Psychology of EQ*

*"What we feel is a choice."*

*— Piyush Shrivastav*

Have you ever seen someone go from mildly upset to uncontrollably enraged? They completely lose it, and you watch helplessly as all rational thoughts leave their mind. On a recent flight from Chicago to Los Angeles, I saw this happen firsthand…

A gentleman in his early sixties was sitting in the aisle seat next to me. A passenger in the seat behind him was placing his luggage in the overhead compartment. Apparently he had bumped my neighbor in the head while stowing his luggage, and my neighbor seemed to be a little annoyed about it. A few minutes later, the man behind us realized that he forgot to grab his newspaper and while getting up, he accidentally bumped the guy again.

This time the man next to me didn't let it go. His face turned red; he turned around and began to yell at the guy for bumping him twice. He reached over the seat and ripped the newspaper out of his hand. He took the newspaper, aggressively folded it, and placed it under his arm. "THAT'S THE SECOND TIME YOU BUMPED ME!" he yelled.

The plane had started pulling away from the jet bridge and we were now heading toward the runway. "Give me back my newspaper NOW!" the man behind us yelled.

I could see a flight attendant look at us from the front of the plane.

"Sir, you can't do that," I said.

Now both flight attendants at the front of the plane were looking in our direction, and one was getting up. "Sir, please listen to me. If you do not give that man his newspaper back, they're going to turn this plane around and escort you off. Look, the flight attendant is coming. You might even get arrested. Is that what you want to happen? Or do you want to just go home?"

To my relief, that warning worked and he was able to calm down enough to realize he was making a big mistake.

"Is there a problem here?" the flight attendant asked.

"No," I said. "We are good. Just some miscommunication is all."

My neighbor returned the newspaper to the gentleman, mumbled a few words and we continued on our flight home without any further incidents.

In the heat of the moment, my neighbor didn't consider the consequences of what might have happened if he ripped the newspaper out of the passenger's hand before he reacted.

When stress triggers the brain's amygdalae (emotion-regulating gray matter inside each cerebral hemisphere) to engage, it releases a steroid called cortisol that can hijack your neocortex (the rational thinking part of the brain). That's because the human brain can only think of four things at one time. When it comes to coaching sports, I like to think of them as four coaching clipboards, which I'll discuss later.

Some people see themselves as efficient multi-taskers—checking e-mail while talking on the phone, cooking dinner, and performing other tasks. However, the human brain is not designed for taking on many tasks at once, or as commonly referred to as multitasking.

Edward Awh and Edward Vogel, researchers at the University of Oregon, concluded in their research that the human brain is unable to handle more than four tasks at a time. The "multitasking cap" is not affected by the complexity of one's thoughts. Surprisingly, many complex concepts can be retained in short-term memory as simple thoughts.[7]

Stress affects all of us at some point in our lives. The funny thing is, even *positive* events like playing a sport or starting a new job can stress us out.

Stress isn't always a bad thing, though. In some cases, it protects us from danger—in fact, that's the whole point of it. Stress is a leftover survival

---

[7] McDougall, Paul. "Humans Can Only Think About Four Things At Once, Study Says." InformationWeek.

technique that we don't have as much of use for now. When we commonly fought for survival, our fight-or-flight mode (triggered by stress) was imperative. These days, the problem comes with having more stress in our lives than we need. Since we rarely *need* to be in fight-or-flight mode, our body's stress reactions can become problematic when they're too strong or happen too often. Since sports put us in the same realm of "survival mode," we need to learn how to handle our gut reactions to it.

Our perception of stress is highly individualized. What rattles your friend's nerves may not faze you, and vice versa. In other words, what matters most is not *what happens* to you, but *how you react* to what happens to you. Let's look at the scientific explanations to show how stress affects us.

**Shuts Down Digestion**
Because our bodies want to use all of our available energy for fighting or fleeing, it stops other energy-spending processes like digestion. This can make us feel nauseous by stopping digestion of the food we've got in our bodies already. Sometimes our bodies even flush the food out with fluids, which turns into vomit. Now we know why we often feel sick before big games or under extreme high-pressure situations.

**Hampers Thinking**

You've probably felt how fast your heart can beat during stressful situations. What's really interesting about this is that your fast heartbeat actually sends a signal to your brain's prefrontal neocortex—the part that handles thought processing and decision-making. The signal tells this part of your brain to shut down temporarily and let your midbrain take over. When we're in this state, instinct and training take over rational thoughts and reasoning. Every person experiences bumps in their relationships—and even the best teams certainly aren't immune to that.[8]

## A CHAMPIONSHIP THAT ALMOST WASN'T

In 2002, the University of Wisconsin Stevens Point women's basketball team sat anxiously waiting to see if they would receive one of the seven at-large bids to the Division 3 NCAA tourney. They all jumped up and cheered as they heard they would host the first round game. After a pretty easy first game route, the team was rewarded with a date to play four-time national champion, Washington University, St. Louis, which was number one in the nation and on a 70-game win streak. To say Wash U was the favorite was a understatement.

---

[8] "The Negative Effects of High Cortisol." Women's Health Network. Accessed January 26, 2018.
https://www.womentowomen.com/emotions-anxiety-mood/stress-and-happiness/.

But then something took place before the game that may have helped change the outcome. Former Pointers player Dianne Hawkins gave me a little insight to what happened:

> "As we got the at-large bid, all the news outlets kept asking us how it felt to get in…[then] it was all about how we felt about being placed in a bracket with Wash U. […] To us the questions should have been about how we were prepping to beat them, but it seemed like the world thought we were done and we thrived on that. It was never talked about *if* we could beat them among us. It was always about *how* we were going to beat them."

When they arrived at the Hoosiers-style gym, the home team kept shouting "Go Bears!" and "Yeah Bears!" in the echoing building. The Pointer team was quiet, mentally preparing, although they were annoyed by the opposing team's raucous nature.

> "Once we got there and got in that gym for pregame and all that chatter started, it was annoying and yet calming because it brought us together more."

That little "annoying" thing brought the team closer—and they ended up beating Wash U, bringing their 70-game win streak to an end on their home court.

Because of that huge win, they were picked by the NCAA to host the Sweet 16 and Elite 8 games. After beating the number-one team in the nation, they were full of confidence. They won those next two games and eventually went on to play St. Lawrence in the national championship game.

> "It was a highly competitive game and both teams were battling back and forth. But pressure has a way of rearing its ugly head at the most inopportune time, [especially] to people if you are not prepared to handle it."

In the final seconds of the game up by 2 points, a Pointer player panicked while trying to inbound the ball, launching the ball across the court instead of calling a time-out as her coach suggested. A St. Lawrence player secured the ball, dribbled, and let it fly.

> "It was straight as an arrow…right on target… And BAM…it hit the back of the rim and bounced out. [We] were national champions."

The University of Wisconsin players were extremely lucky because of the St. Lawrence player's missed shot. But why did that Pointer player not listen to the coach and instead throw the ball? It wasn't that she didn't listen or wanted to make a mistake. It was the dreaded *amygdala hijack*.

The pressure of potentially winning or losing a national championship game caused her neocortex to essentially shut down. She forgot she had a time-out and forgot what the coach told her to do. Basically she couldn't think clearly and made a huge mistake. It almost cost her team the national championship. Let's look at how this happened.

When stress happens, how do some people instinctively know how to keep their emotions in check? Stress and the brain are closely linked.

There are three parts of the brain that are highly involved in how we recognize and respond to stressors:

- The amygdala
- The hippocampus
- The prefrontal neocortex

These three areas of the brain work with the hypothalamus to turn on and off the production of stress hormones (adrenaline, noradrenaline, and cortisol) and related responses like an increased heart rate.[9] Apart from controlling our stress response, our brain can also be affected *by* the stress itself.

---

[9] Tucker, Whitney. "The Science of Stress." Armed Science. http://science.dodlive.mil/2013/08/26/the-science-of-stress/.

Researchers are now learning how stressors can physically alter our brain and brain functions, which may impact how we learn, form memories, and even make decisions. In the following explanation I will use "clipboards" as a visual guide since we are talking about coaching. Each number (1, 2, 3, 4) will represent a single clipboard or thought that you can have when you are under no stress. Because the brain can only handle four thoughts (clipboards) at one time, there is also a limited amount of responses that we can think about under non-stress conditions.[10] According to J.P. Pawliw-Fry, that limited amount of responses is defined by the factorial of the number of clipboards your brain is handling at that time.

Therefore, under non-stressful conditions, if the brain has the capacity to hold four "clipboards" at one time, it can come up with four-factorial (4) responses/solutions to a problem, which is 4 x 3 x 2 x 1 = 24. Twenty-four is the maximum amount of thoughts or "solutions" we can make to handle a non-stressful problem.[11]

Let's say I'm in an argument with someone. Stress enters the equation and I get upset or "lose a clipboard." Now I only have three left. Because I lost one of my four clipboards, it looks like I have lost

---

[10] Burrows, Betty. "How Stress Works." HowStuffWorks Science. http://science.howstuffworks.com/life/inside-the-mind/human-brain/how-stress-works.htm.
[11] Pawliw-Fry, JP. "Emotional Intelligence." Keynote speech, Green Bay, WI, 2014.

25% of my rational thought process because I only have three clipboards left...but in reality, the new factorial equation is 3 x 2 x 1 = 6. Six is the new number of how many solutions I can have to my problem. So instead of being able to think of 24 different solutions to my problem, I can only think of six!

I have *not* lost 25% of my rational thought...but rather 75% of it. If this situation becomes more stressful and I lose another clipboard, then the numbers become much more black and white: 2 x 1 = 2. Now, it's me versus you; we are probably screaming at each other and don't care who's watching or what others think of the situation. If you lose all of your "clipboards," the confrontation might turn physical—and that's when bad things can happen. All rational thought is out the door because the amygdala has completely hijacked the neocortex.

Once this happens, it takes eighteen minutes for the brain to calm down and get rid of the cortisol so you can recover your clipboards. Let's look at another example of how this plays into the world of sports.

The Cincinnati Bengals lost a huge playoff game in the 2015–2016 season because they let the stress of the moment get to them. They were dropping "clipboards" quickly. Here is an account of that game from Chris Chase, a NFL beat writer for FTW (For the Win).[12]

---

12 Chase, Chris. "Blame Marvin Lewis for Cincinnati's out-of-

*"After a Pittsburgh interception with 1:50 remaining, the game looked locked up—Cincinnati's first playoff win since 1990—right up until Jeremy Hill fumbled the ball on Cincinnati's first carry after the turnover. Ben Roethlisberger, who had exited the game earlier with a shoulder injury (caused by Burfict – which is why he stayed in the game; he's a stud on the field), then returned, needing at least 50 yards to get his Steelers in position for a game-winning field goal. It quickly became clear Roethlisberger didn't have the arm to make big plays, so a slow march it was. At that pace it appeared Pittsburgh might have the time to get into position, but the odds were going to be about as long as the kick.*

*Enter Vontaze Burfict. After a Roethlisberger pass to Antonio Brown was overthrown by about five yards, Burfict sprinted in, a good second or two after the play, headhunting all the way. He received a 15-yard penalty and was lucky not to be ejected. Later, Adam Jones touched a ref while trying to get involved in a scrum and gave away another 15 yards. (To be fair, Pacman's penalty was touchy. He looked like he was going at Steelers assistant Joey Porter, not an official. Given the level of discourse during the game, it was a flag that could have been swallowed. But when you play like the Bengals*

control playoff ..." For the Win.
http://ftw.usatoday.com/2016/01/marvin-lewis-vontaze-burfict-cincinnati-bengals-loss-adam-jones-pittsburgh-steelers-fired.

*did for 58 minutes and you have the history that Pacman does, you don't get the benefit of the doubt.)*

*In all, the undisciplined Bengals gave Pittsburgh 30 yards and a chip-shot field goal to win. Those 30 yards weren't going to be easy to come by, not with a quarterback who could barely lift his arm in a driving downpour. But the Steelers were handed them on a black and orange platter. A field goal later and it was 18-16 Steelers and, essentially, the game.*

*And now the 25-year playoff-losing streak continues in Cincinnati. Again, Burfict and Jones are the selfish children whose actions lost the game."[13]*

As you can see, emotional intelligence makes up a huge part of the sporting world. Games can be won and lost because someone has better control of their emotions and can think more clearly than those who don't. A big part of having better control of one's emotions is by using self-talk.

## USE SELF-TALK – DON'T PANIC

Don't panic—communicate with yourself and you'll succeed. This is an important part of the pillar of Self-Talk.

---

13 Ibid.

Dave, a bar manager, was my boss while I attended college at the University of Wisconsin Stevens Point. He is as close to me and in many aspects even closer to me than my own father. Dave is also one of the toughest guys I have ever met. One evening, Dave came back from an ice fishing trip with a look on his face I had never seen before. It was a look that had a mix of shock, fear, and relief all rolled into one. I immediately knew something serious had happened.

Dave and a friend (Jack) decided to spend the day ice fishing on the river. Just in case you have never heard of ice fishing before, it gets so cold in the winter where I live in Wisconsin that lakes and rivers freeze over with a thick sheet of ice. In fact, it gets so thick that you can drive full-size vehicles and park them on it. It's normally extremely safe as long as you are not near fast-moving water or close to springtime when temperatures are warmer and ice thaws. Neither factor was in play on this particular day.

Dave and Jack arrived early in the morning and unloaded the four-wheeler from the back of the truck, packed up all of their gear and headed out for their fishing site. After spending most of the day on the ice, it was getting dark and they decided to call it a day and head back to the truck. What they didn't know was that at some point during the day the river had shifted the ice and caused a big hole to open up. The hole had been exposed to the cold long enough that it had already started to freeze over again, but it had not been long enough to make it safe to drive on.

They were traveling back along the exact same route in the dark when they hit the weak ice. Without warning, both of them were thrown into the water—and a battle for survival began. Since Jack was sitting on the back, he was launched the farthest away from the vehicle and Dave was flipped directly underneath the four-wheeler. He specifically recounted his immediate thoughts to me:

> "Because it was dark, I couldn't see the thin ice. One minute I was driving and the next minute I was under water. I could feel the four-wheeler above me and I was trying to kick it away so I didn't get trapped underneath it. Then I tried to grab onto it and pull myself on top of it, but it just kept spinning in the water. I couldn't see a thing and my fear was starting to turn into panic. But I knew that if I continued to panic, I was dead!"

The next decision Dave made probably saved his life. Dave calmed himself down by repeating in his head, "Don't panic, Dave. Don't panic. If you panic, you are dead."

He said that as soon as he thought those words, he was able to calm down and regain his composure. Dave was able to "self-talk" to calm himself down in the most intense situation he had ever been in.

After successfully pushing himself away from the four-wheeler, he had to orient himself in the pitch-black water. It's not uncommon for people who are in this position to swim in the wrong direction because they lose their orientation and drown.

His composure now regained, he realized that he could hear Jack's voice screaming for him. It was his friend's voice that gave him direction. Now he knew which way was up. As luck would have it, Jack was thrown far enough to be right next to the thicker ice and he was able to hold on to it while he yelled for Dave. Once Dave resurfaced, he grabbed the back of Jack's boots and they were able to help each other get out of the water. They had a long cold walk back to their truck, but at least they were alive.

I don't know how many of us would have been able to control our emotions when thrown into deep freezing water, much less in the dark, all while trapped under a quad. However, Dave was able to remain calm under the most stressful of circumstances and find his way out.

Most sports teams don't realize that they are panicking and "swimming" in the wrong direction. They don't have the EQ skills to calm themselves down and succeed. It's incredibly important to develop strong EQ self-communication skills so team members can learn not to "drown."

The following five steps will allow you to access your emotional intelligence.

1. **Make a Decision.** In order for any of the information that I am about to share with you to be effective, you have to *decide* that you want to become a better person, friend, coach and teammate. Until you decide that you want to grow as a person, it's impossible to grow as a team. You can start by asking yourself the following questions (from Boyatzis' Theory of Self-Directed Learning):

- My ideal self: Who do I want to be?
- My real self: Who am I? What are the strengths and gaps in my personality?
- My learning agenda: How can I build on my strengths while reducing my gaps?

Once you answer these questions about yourself and understand your necessary learning areas, experiment with new behaviors, thoughts, and feelings to the point of mastery, you will be able to focus on developing supportive, trusting relationships that make change possible.

Intentional Change Model ©Richard E. Boyatzis, 2006

2. **Ask Yourself the Tough Questions.**
   Coaches and players should ask themselves
   these emotional intelligence questions and
   answer as honestly as possible. Asking these
   questions requires emotional self-awareness in
   order to answer them honestly.

- Would you recruit *you*?
- Would you want *you* for a teammate?
- Would you want to play for *you*?
- What do people like about your personality?
- What do people dislike about your personality
  or what deficiencies have caused you to lose
  friends?
- Would you want to work for *you*?
- Can you delay gratification or are you
  someone who wants instant returns without
  putting in the daily or weekly activity
  necessary for results?
- Are you taking time to develop relationships
  with teammates and staff?

- What's your attitude like when adversity hits?

- Under which circumstances are you a winner or a whiner?

3. **Plan for Your Success.** You have probably heard a saying like this at some point in your life, "Choose your friends wisely." Hang around the type of people you want to be like. You are the average of your five closest friends. Involve yourself with positive, emotionally intelligent people and you will find yourself becoming more aware of your actions. If you seek out successful people and add them to your inner circle, you will be more likely to learn how they became successful.

4. **Manage Your Emotions.** Good teams manage their emotions by managing their self-talk. Self-talk is what you say to yourself; it can be either positive or negative. Keep in mind that whatever you say to yourself becomes a self-fulfilling prophecy. In other words, it becomes your TRUTH!

5. **Get an Accountability Partner.** Hold each other accountable, and be willing to be held

accountable by others. This is one of the toughest things for a person to do on both fronts, but teams that are willing to have your flaws critiqued create a much stronger bond because of the trust that is built.

# TALKING POINTS

*Q: What is the amygdala and how does it affect us?*

*Q; What is an amygdala hijack?*

*Q: What strategy would you use to calm yourself down in a stressful situation??*

- the amygdala is a part of the brain it can affect you when you are stressed and not thinking straignt.

- when you have a win or lose situation on the line and you forget what you were told before.

- count my fingers take a few breathes

# CHAPTER 5
*Relationship Management*

*"If you do not have control over your mouth, you will not have control over your future."*

— Germany Kent

Relationship management is using the awareness of your own emotions and the emotions of others to manage interactions successfully. It involves clear communication and effective handling of conflict. It's the bond you build with others over time.

Building a solid relationship is something that should be cherished. Strong relationships are the result of the history you share with others, how you treat them, and how you understand them. The weaker your relationship with someone, the less likely you are going to be able to get your point across to them.

The hardest thing to do is manage a relationship during times of stress. Stress can cause us to shut down and not want to communicate, or it can cause us to blow up and say things that we normally wouldn't say.

**4 Tips for Effective Relationship Management:**

1. **Know that Timing is Everything.** Patience is critical. Managing relationships can be very difficult, so it's very important to find the right time to talk. Sometimes, it's better to wait until time has passed and everyone is calm. But the only way you will know that is by spending time with that person and really try to get to know them.

2. **Understand that the Person is Most Likely Motivated by Hurt.** If someone is angry, try to understand that they're hurt or sad underneath the anger. Instead of responding with aggression, seek to understand what it is that hurt them and respond to that. Then, validate their feelings and comfort them while looking at how you may have contributed to the problem.

3. **Think about What You're About to Say.** Be mindful of your approach; think about what it means to say something before actually saying it. Learning how to argue in a calm, respectful, and considerate way will ensure that you don't cross a boundary from which you cannot return.

4. **Pay Attention to Your Tone of Voice and Body Language.** Sometimes bringing up problems has to be done softly, compassionately, and in a non-threatening way. Emotionally intelligent people are mindful of their tone and how they present concerns and issues. Make sure to keep your arms uncrossed and open. Open body language will allow the person to feel more comfortable with you and it will also help to ease tensions.

## THE IMPORTANCE OF BUILDING TRUST

Trust is one of the hardest things to gain from someone. Most of us are fortunate enough to have people in our lives that we trust—but what is it exactly that allows us to trust someone? As humans, we generally trust someone who is reliable and consistent in their actions. Another important aspect of building trust is being likable.

Think about the people in your life that you trust the most. What are the qualities that make you trust them? Liking someone and enjoying their company is usually on the list.

Unfortunately, the people you trust aren't always likable. When I was an athlete, my coach would push me hard in practice or say things to motivate me. Although I didn't always like him for it at the time, he was always consistent with his honesty about my performance and that is why I still love and respect him today.

In order to become likable among others, you have to first become transparent. A major obstacle to overcome in achieving transparency to become likable and build trust is to accept yourself—both your strengths and your weaknesses. Doing so will help you become more comfortable with yourself and your abilities.

Five traits to build trust and likability include friendliness, relevance, empathy, realness, and authenticity and confidence.

**Friendliness:** Are you approachable? Do you smile and engage others? Are you interested in other people's personal and professional lives? Do you go out of your way to introduce yourself to others?

**Relevance:** Whom have you helped in the last month? More importantly, why did you help them? Did you have the opportunity to help someone and didn't? Under which circumstances are you a giver or a taker?

**Empathy:** Do you try to understand other people's perspectives? Do you listen more than you speak?

**Realness:** Are you genuine in words and actions? Do you show up as the real deal?

**Authenticity and Confidence:** Another key trait that a likable person has is authenticity. When you are authentic with someone, you are more likely to gain their trust. Another key component to being authentic is confidence. Confidence comes from *knowing* that you are prepared and believing in yourself because of it. If you put in hours of practice needed to master your craft (no matter what it is), it will allow you to relax and just be yourself.

# TALKING POINTS

*Q: What mistakes do people make managing their relationships?*

*Q: Give an example of a time when you had to deal with a difficult co-worker or teammate. How did you handle the situation? Would you handle it differently now?*

- stress and not putting there feet in someone else's shoes.

- well I didn't but, my volleyball team had a huge fight with this one girl and are whole volleyball team didn't like for it but at the time I didn't know what was going on but, when I did I knew what she did was just probably her emotions and still became her friend.

# CHAPTER 6
*Social Awareness*

*"Walk with me for a while, my friend – you in my shoes, I in yours – and then let us talk."*

*– Richelle E. Goodrich*

Understanding other people's feelings is a central part of emotional intelligence. Interacting with others, especially in a coaching or team player position, is critical. When emotions are inevitably thrown into the mix, things can get tedious. How do you react when you have a stubborn player? What do you say to the coach who is just too harsh? If you get it wrong, you can be seen as uncaring or insensitive. Get it right and you might have a friend for life.

With the rising popularity of social media, we tend to be less caring and have less empathy for each other. It's much easier to talk bad about someone when you hide behind a keyboard and don't have to do it directly to their face. If you don't like someone's comments you can simply log off or "un-friend" them without face to face interaction.

This has far-reaching issues, however. In today's world of online presence, people are losing their human touch.

The problem with lack of empathy is that it leads to a lack of understanding of what a person needs.

When you are not giving people what they need, it can lead to an erosion of trust. Listening is critical; *learning* to listen for feelings is even more important.

People don't always directly express their true feelings. Some people, especially men, have difficulty expressing their emotions; others don't even *understand* their own emotions. *Pay attention.* Listen with the intent to validate that their viewpoint is legitimate. *Put yourself in their shoes* and ask yourself, "How would I feel if I had this problem?" This will go a long way in building a deeper level of trust with them.

Most successful leaders maintain self-control, remain grounded when things get tough, and know when to make decisions quickly and decisively. But on the other side, a leader also knows when to step back and think a decision through.

A successful leader is empathetic, listens carefully, and tries to understand what a person is saying and feeling. They are also a *great* communicator. They rely on training to make the best possible decision at the right time. Most of all, they understand that they don't know everything; they'll admit when they are wrong and are not afraid to fail.

When a particular player does not respond well to critiques, there could be underlying factors that prevent them from dealing with those issues. Emotional intelligence allows coaches and players to find underlying factors that might hinder their growth as a player, person, and professional. Usually, a hidden factor is the culprit of why someone will not buy into the direction a program wants to go. It may also be the reason a player or coach is not performing optimally.

My teammate Chad was the first junior captain in the history of our program. He was not the most talented player on our team, but was the true definition of a leader. Chad always found a way to get the job done and he was tough as nails. When we needed a big play, it was typically Chad who was in the middle of making it happen.

One day during practice, our coach challenged his leadership and Chad lost his cool, big time! F-bombs were thrown around; he picked up some metal bleachers and slammed them on the gym floor as he screamed back at our coach. Chad had lost it. Our entire practice came to a screeching halt as he stormed out of the gym.

Our coach didn't like outward displays of negative emotion. Facial expressions or eye rolling and especially swearing of any kind were not tolerated, much less slamming bleachers and storming out of the gym screaming back at the coach.

My immediate thought was, "Oh no, Chad is going to get kicked off the team. Our season is over."

But not everyone knew that his mom was an alcoholic and was slowly dying from her disease. None of us could relate to what Chad was going through. Rather than yell at Chad and berate him for making such a spectacle, my coach was able to see that he probably had pushed Chad too hard that day, and made up for that mistake by speaking to Chad the next day. He was emotionally intelligent enough to see that Chad's reaction was out of character. He talked with him and they worked the problem out.

Some coaches would have handled that situation much differently. It's easy to get angry; our coach could have easily kicked Chad off the team. But cooler heads prevailed and we went on to have an amazing season, largely in part to his leadership. Emotional intelligence eventually won out.

Chad's story is a great segue into leadership, another important concept in the success of a sports team.

## TALKING POINTS

*Q: Why is social awareness so important?*

*Q: How can you build social awareness?*

- you never know what other people are going threw and better to try to see what other people are going through.

- by not assuming and try to step in someone else's shoes.

# CHAPTER 7
*Misconceptions of Leadership*

There are two common mistakes people make about leadership. Too often someone thinks that in order to be a leader they need someone to *tell them* when to be a leader. But you do not have to wait. All you have to do is take action and decide you are going to be a leader.

The first thing to understand about leadership is that in order to lead, you have to find out what people want. *And what people want is to feel like they are appreciated and that when they leave they are going to be missed.* When you are missed, it means you impacted someone in a good way. When you are appreciated, it means you bring a certain value to the team that everyone loves about you.

Another misconception is that people think you have to have a special kind of personality to lead. You don't need a special kind of personality to lead—it's actually the opposite. By becoming a leader, you can naturally change your personality. I believe you can build an "alter-ego."

Here are some characteristics of great leaders:

- They challenge what is considered to be the status quo.
- They build a culture or a language, a way of knowing if you are in or out.
- They have curiosity about people *inside* and *outside* their group.
- They bring people together.
- They commit to a common cause or purpose.

## QUESTIONS LEADERS CAN ASK TO HELP PLAYERS AND THEMSELVES DEVELOP EQ

This is a small list of questions leaders should ask themselves and players to develop EQ:

- What do I do well and how do I repeat it?
- What do I do that might hinder my growth and the team's growth?
- Am I willing to hold teammates or coaching staff accountable?
- Am I willing to be held accountable?
- What can I do better or differently to improve my skills in EQ?
- Am I willing to listen to hard truths about my flaws and be coachable?

- Who else has a skill set I need to learn from?
- Who can I talk to that would understand my problem?

Once these questions are answered, have the players share their skill and thought process behind it. Make the player feel like an expert by having them teach that skill to other players. Maybe someone has a great study skill that other teammates could benefit from. Maybe someone has fantastic footwork and runs a route better than anyone else. Also, leaders should be open to sharing their own strengths and listen to critiques about their weakness.

While you're at it, make an effort to build team norms. For instance, group emotional intelligence is about those small acts that can make a big difference. It's not always about working or practicing all night, it is about saying 'thankyou' for choosing to do so. It is not always about having in-depth discussions on performance and strategy, it is about asking a quiet colleague about their thoughts. In this way, true leaders are able to create harmony and minimize stress, while making every team member know that they are valued.

When I complete these exercises, my goal is to give everyone a role on the team that they can be proud of. This includes team managers and volunteers. When a person feels like they have ownership, they are more willing to take pride in the values and success of the team. But the most important exercise of all is that leaders need to ask themselves the same questions they ask the players. "Why," you ask?

*"Quality questions create a quality life. Successful people ask better questions, and as a result, they get better answers."*
*-Tony Robbins*

As a leader, the most important task you have is to lead by example. You need to perform at your best consistently so you are able to inspire and motivate your team. Before determining the benchmark for excellence in the lives of others, a leader needs to reach that mark themselves. It's hard to do, which is why great leaders are always up for a challenge. While leadership isn't to be misunderstood with management, it's still important for a leader to be there whenever their team needs them. This transformation won't happen instantly, but with a plan and support system it can be achieved.

The girls' basketball coach at a high school I used to coach at had three different colored whistles that he would rotate for practice every day. Before practice, he would select the one that matched his mood for the day. If he wore the red whistle, it meant he was upset and that his players should expect a very tough practice. If he wore a green one, it meant that he was in a good mood and typically practice would be easier. And if he wore a black whistle, it meant that he was neutral and it could go either way.

When he first told me about this, I laughed because I thought he was joking. But then he reached inside his desk drawer and pulled them out. I immediately stopped laughing because I didn't want him to put the red whistle on while I was sitting there.

In theory, I guess it would be great if we all wore something that would quickly help identify what kind of mood we are in. But in reality, he was being selfish. The focus was all about him and he was only making his players care more about his mood rather than learning basketball skills. They were being taught to fear practice if he was wearing a red whistle or relax if he was wearing a green one. I wondered what would happen if he were wearing a green whistle when his mood changed? I pictured him stopping practice to switch whistles when someone did something he didn't like!

It's hard to manage anyone if you can't manage yourself. That coach was an inconsistent leader; he couldn't contain and manage his emotions. And from a coaching perspective, when I watched his team play, they were extremely inconsistent as well. Below are the steps to help you become a more consistent leader.

## LEADERSHIP ACTION PLAN

1. **Be Transparent.** Inconsistent behavior is strongly related to poor impulse control. A player or coach may say things without fully

thinking them through. They may have a wide variety of emotional gut reactions and frequently let them out. If your peers or coaching staff have to constantly wonder what kind of mood or what kind of effort you are going to bring into practice every day, chances are you're not showing up ready to lead.

2. **Be Consistent.** When you are a leader, you give up the right to have mood swings. You are automatically held to a higher standard by your coaches and peers, but more importantly, you hold *yourself* to a higher standard.

Be consistent in your attitude and your efforts inside and out of practice. During downtime, think about the times that you might be challenged to handle your emotions in practice or in a game. Visit a past stressful situation and think about how you would handle it differently if it came up again. The pace of the leader creates the pace of the team, and how you handle the day-to-day challenges of a season is how the team will handle those challenges as well.

3. **Use Positive Self-Talk.** We all have doubts and insecurities, and we often let that lead into negative self-talk. It can get worse if more things don't go right for us. "*I suck,*" "*I*

*can't do anything right today,"* and *"I want to quit"* are phrases people allow themselves to say when things get bad. So why not change the negative talk to positive talk?

No one can stop you from thinking positive thoughts in your own mind.

Say, *"I am in control right now; I am not going to quit. I am good. I am not going to let my anger beat me"* when your emotions are put to the test. Trust me—I know how corny it sounds. But believe it or not, it actually works. No matter what it is, it's important to use the words *"I am"* because your subconscious mind believes what it is repeatedly told.

Your body and its senses will believe what your mind tells it. You saw a good example of this in the ice fishing story earlier in the book: Dave was able to control his emotions by using self-talk to remain calm and not panic.

4. **Set High Expectations.** Raise the standard for effort and mental toughness by showing them that you are willing to do whatever it takes to win. If that means pushing your teammates when things aren't going well, so be it. If it means you are the loudest voice on the sideline, so be it. Don't be afraid to *hold* them accountable and don't be afraid to be *held* accountable when the situation presents

itself. It has to work *both ways* for this to be effective. *Leadership is not a one-way street.*

Be sure that your actions align with your words—because if they don't, your team will not respect your leadership and you will not be able to set the standard for your expectations.

Too often, leaders fall into the assumption that they need to always be liked in order for their peers to listen to them. There is a difference between being liked and being respected. One gets you invited to a party and the other gets people to come to your party. Your teammates may like you, but they only value your input and will allow you to push them if they respect you.

Notice the words I used there: "will allow." The tone in which you choose to communicate with your teammates is extremely important. There is a fine line between pushing a teammate and being a condescending jerk.

*"Anyone can become angry – that is easy, but to be angry with the right person, to the right degree, at the right time for the right purpose and in the right way – that is not within everyone's power and is not easy."*

*– Aristotle*

Pay attention to the brilliance of this quote and see how much emotional intelligence is interwoven within it.

5. **Mentor the Younger Generation.** Teaching is a privilege. Someone trusts you enough to put you in charge of a learning environment and others are allowing you to teach them. Both come with huge responsibilities. When you have an opportunity to make a difference in someone's confidence, attitude, skillset, and life—do not take it for granted.

If you value what your program has given you and you value what others have done before you, make sure you teach those same principles to the next generation. They are the ones who will maintain high EQ standards for the program's continued success.

6. **Don't Forget to Have Fun.** Leadership also means being able to let go and relax. Don't forget to have fun even if there are tough times. Find the funny in a bad situation. Sometimes we all need to lighten up and learn how to laugh and have fun again. Being consistent also means being able to have fun when a situation calls for it, but it also means that you are able to get back to business when the moment is over. Set up times for the team to get together for video game

tournaments, ping-pong matches, or anything that will bring your team together. It's important for your team to have fun and relieve the stress of practice and school. Let the fun side of your personality shine at the right moments.

A good friend of mine was a former director of basketball operations at the University of Iowa. He used to tell all of the coaches that if you decide to go out at night and have fun, you had better be able to "burn the candle at both ends." In laymen's terms, "have as much fun as you want, but you better not let it affect the quality of your work."

The very best teams that I have talked to have as much fun as every other team—they just do it differently. They have *responsible* fun and don't put themselves or their teammates into situations that can be bad for the program. They know the fine line between fun and being irresponsible and do not cross it. The season is really long and very stressful—so don't forget to work at having fun!

7. **Apply Servant Leadership.** My wife and I decided that when our children were old enough, we were going to teach them the

value of giving. We decided the best way to do this was to break up the money they received for birthdays or Christmas into thirds. One third would go into a college account, one third they could use to buy whatever they wanted, and the last third would be given to a charity of their choice.

They could give as much or as little as they wanted of that third to the charity. After I returned home from a business trip, my wife had a really neat story to tell me about my oldest son Ben.

One day my wife and Ben were having a discussion about a family in need. After learning about their troubles he asked if he could give some of his money to this family. My wife was really excited because this was the first time he wanted to donate. She retrieved his money and emptied all of the change and bills from his charity piggy bank on the kitchen table. She grabbed a small plastic bag and watched him as he sat there separating his money into its own little "donate" pile. As she watched him, she began to notice that he was pushing all of the pennies away from the rest of his change and began to put all of the pennies inside the bag. As I sat listening to my wife tell me the story I immediately thought, "Well...it's not very much, but for his first time it's okay." But when he handed my wife the bag of pennies, he said, "Here, Mom, I'm giving you all of the gold ones because they are worth the most!"

It wasn't until many months later when I was telling this story to my friend that I really got the message.

I had inadvertently judged my own son.

By today's standards, a penny is almost worthless, so in my mind I felt like he should have been giving more. In reality, however, something of much greater importance was happening: the value of servant leadership. It seemed to me that he was giving the least, but in Ben's eyes, he was giving the most he possibly could.

Instead of thinking that the more things of "value" we give, the better person we are, look at the "value" of the meaning. It's not the amount that should be the area of focus; it's the *meaning* behind it.

In the end, the idea is to establish positive norms so that the team as a whole is able to also have empathy, both internally and externally. Not individually, but as a team. A true leader is able to create an environment where they are able to articulate a shared mission that resonates with the rest of the team. This is only possible if one is able to tune into their own values, tune into the values of others in a team, and lead authentically. The goal is to become a resonate leader instead of a dissonant leader, who doesn't care about how people feel and uses fear as a motivator.

By helping release positive energies in your team, it increases the energy that's available to them, which, in turn, puts the team in a state where they are able to perform at their best.

## Resonant Leadership
## vs.
## Dissonant Leadership

Good managers have many traits in common. Organization, delegation, prioritization, and communication are just some of the skills that all good managers possess.

But the key skill that separates good managers from great ones is a quality called leadership. Few people know this but there are two types of leaders at the workplace—resonate and dissonant leaders.

A resonate leader is one who is focused on the emotional wellbeing of their team. These leaders emphasize the importance of building core values and personal growth as well as the importance of completing projects successfully. A resonate leader is the one who does not just lead a team, they inspire loyalty and help drive teamwork.

On the other side of the spectrum stands the dissonant leader. This person is more focused on achieving goals and growing the company, rather than spending time nurturing their team members. A dissonant leader is characterized as a leader who avoids democratic practices in order to keep things moving or avoid stalemates. A dissonant leader is most effective in times of crisis since they have a pigeon hole focus on the task at hand without getting into the emotional side of being a leader and the relationship that a manager has with their team. In other words, they don't let their feelings get in the way of an important task. Resonant leaders score higher on emotional intelligence and have a better ability to connect with their followers because they show empathy with the ones who may be struggling with life challenges. These leaders are more likely to create harmony in the workplace. Employees believe that a resonant leader cares as much for them as for their work performance. Resonant leaders are coaches, visionaries, and democratic leaders. While this leadership style is charismatic and transformational though at the extreme, this style could lead to poor discipline or inefficiency.

Dissonant leaders, on the other hand, remain objective and logical in decision making. This type of leadership can lead to stress, emotional frustration, and burnout of employees. This approach is viewed by employees as distant and cold. A dissonant leadership style operates in a highly authoritative style and can be useful in crunch time, but it can wear on employees.

# TALKING POINTS

*Q: List a few characteristics of a great leader. Do you possess any of those characteristics in your own leadership style?*

*Q: What do you think is a weakness in your leadership style?*

- There motivating, helpful, easy to talk to
humble. I do I just don't use them
as much.

- my quiet ness and my negativity
towards myself.

# CHAPTER 8
*EQ for Coaches*

All people really want is to feel that they are a part of a family. This is not different for your players and staff. But in today's world, high school and college sports have become more like a business. If you don't produce wins and do it quickly enough, you lose your "business."

A great way to view a sports program is that of how you view a family business. You have the closeness of a family-operated business that helps you run it, and not just typical "employees." Just like in your home life, it takes a lot of hard work to keep a family together. If you don't put in the effort to keep building stronger relationships with your players or staff, they will not want to put in a consistent effort to help the program grow. Both will not live up to their potential—or worse: They will both fail!

In any sport, you want to create a culture within your program that makes your players know that you care. Some of the coaches I have met treat their players like a "vendorship"—they only find value based on what's good for them. It gets even worse when they treat their "star" players differently and everyone else is treated just like a vendorship. The really good coaches treat their players like a partnership—they mutually benefit from each other.

There's nothing wrong with coaches wanting to win, but sometimes the stress of having to win can lead coaches into making bad decisions for their players and their program.

Sometimes pressure can cause a coach to forget that his main purpose in coaching is to prepare their players for life. Learning about EQ will help coaches to learn impulse control, manage stress, and know when to listen more than talk.

Emotionally intelligent coaches know how to push the "hot button" in people. They understand that there are different types of personalities on a team and use this knowledge to motivate them. Some players can be yelled at, some just need to be talked to, and others need very little to remain motivated.

We *all* need different styles of communication to succeed. Understanding an individual's personality, as well as their background story, can be huge for their future growth as a person. If you don't understand what motivates your players, you might turn a kid against you, which can lead to more headaches down the road.

In the movie *Patch Adams*, Patch is a medical student who uses fun, humor, and more importantly empathy to relate to his patients. He understands the human side of his patients and tries to relate to them on a more personal level. Later in the movie, there is a scene where another medical student is having a problem with one of his patients. The student is at the top of his class academically, but lacks the social skills and empathy to connect with his patient. He knows exactly what's wrong with his patient medically, but his bedside manner is awkward and cold. The patient refuses to eat and will not take her medicine simply because she doesn't like him.

The bottom line is, people will not do what you want or go out of their way to help you if they don't like you.

## WHY TO ADD EQ AWARENESS TO YOUR SPORTS PROGRAM

All coaches want athletic, skilled players who have a high IQ in their respective sports. And while this is obviously important, it is definitely not the only thing that determines success. In fact, I believe a player who has a high EQ can trump a player who only has a high sports IQ because they approach their sport in a different way. They understand how his or her actions can affect the team.

A player might struggle because he or she has a lack of communication skills, social awareness skills, or other issues. As stated before, many players come from different social and economic backgrounds. One player might not understand what it was like to live in fear for their life every day walking home from school, while another may never know what it's like to worry about financial hardship.

What every player and coach should understand is that *everyone* has a story. Everyone has different life experiences that shape their personality for the good and the bad. The more you can learn about someone's personal story, the more likely they will allow you to build a meaningful relationship with them.

By developing EQ in your players and program, you will help bridge the gap in communication and strengthen the relationship between teammates, leading to increased wins and a stronger bond among teammates and coaches.

## EVERYONE'S DIFFERENT VIEW OF "WIN"

When I was younger, I used to watch the *And1 Mixed Tape Tour*. While I am a basketball fundamentalist at heart, I still enjoyed the flash and creative style of players like Hot Sauce and The Professor who would use their creativity to entertain crowds with amazing ball-handling skills and theatrical dunks.

During an after-game interview, one of the star players, talked about his dream of making it to an NBA roster. I recall him saying something to the effect of …*My dream? I just want to get on a bench, any bench. Just put me on any bench in the NBA and I will be happy.*

My immediate thought was, *That's why you're not in the NBA*. His vision of a "win" was to just be on the bench…but if you think about Michael Jordan, Venus Williams, or Tom Brady's competitiveness in wanting to win, you would see that they have a completely different view of what a "win" is. Their dream is to win championships, not just "win" by making it to a roster.

Later on in high school, I really took pride in being a good teammate. I knew I was not the most athletic or talented, but I didn't let that get in the way of always trying to get better and accept any role that my coach asked me to fill. I did it because I wanted to win at any cost. After I graduated from high school, I made a decision to stick around southern California and attend College of the Canyons. I wanted to continue playing basketball; this seemed like the perfect opportunity to get physically stronger and develop my skills so I could continue my basketball career at a bigger college one day. Since it was a junior college, you never knew who was going to be on the roster, as the teams can change drastically from year to year.

That year we had a bunch of guys from all over our valley, including a few guys who were from rival high schools. Our rivalries were pretty serious. We never talked to players from opposing schools and they didn't talk to us. To put it plainly, we didn't like each other at all. That dislike for each other carried over into the season. It really showed in practice but especially manifested on the court.

We played harder against each other in practice than we did against opposing teams. But there was *one* player in particular who played exceptionally hard against them. He definitely did not want to lose his spot or have his minutes taken away by those players.

I was that player. Back then, if you had asked me if I wanted to win, I would have said of course, because I *did* want to win. But to what *degree* did I want to win? Now that's a totally different answer. And when I asked myself that question some twenty years later, that was the moment when the truth slapped me across the face. I was now looking back at one of the worst playing experiences of my basketball career and realizing that *I* was a bad teammate. *I* was responsible for some of the lack of chemistry on the team.

We lost over twenty games and I never once blamed myself. I always looked at the coaches and the other guys on the team as the reason we were losing and I blamed them. I never even once considered blaming myself. I didn't want to put aside the high school rivalry I had with a few guys for the betterment of the team—and we lost because of it. Was I the *only* one to blame? No. But if I looked back with honesty, I didn't want to win badly enough. I could have been the bigger person and extended the olive branch for the betterment of the team...but I did not. At that time, I only cared about playing time and—more importantly—playing ahead of them. I didn't want to help them improve because I didn't like them and they didn't like me. I was selfish.

Unfortunately, I didn't realize this until many years later when I asked myself the hard questions about my role as a teammate. It only happened because I learned about emotional intelligence and was able to self-reflect—and more importantly, be honest with myself.

## TEACHING PLAYERS TO BE PROBLEM SOLVERS

Have you ever met someone who really loves his or her role or responsibility? On the other hand, have you met someone who just shows up and does the minimum to keep the position assigned to them?

Teams that score high in emotional intelligence read, listen, and learn because they are constantly trying to improve. Team members are always striving to better themselves personally and professionally. These team players are great at the skill of self-actualization. They realize their talents and have a strong desire for self-fulfillment. A player who self-actualizes is valued more because they are always on a continuous learning curve. He or she doesn't settle for "good enough."

Emotional intelligence teaches players to be problem solvers rather than problem reporters. After one of his players came to him with a problem before practice, a good friend of mine said to him, "Don't come to me with problems; I have enough problems in my life for all of us. Come to me with solutions."

I have since taught this skill to my players. I want to help them become problem solvers. Rather than say, "Hey Coach, my teacher is making me stay after class to finish a project. Can you talk to her and tell her that I can't miss practice?" say, "Hey Coach, here is my problem: My teacher is making me stay after class to finish a project and I was going to have to miss the beginning of practice, but I talked to her and she gave me a couple of different options so I can finish my project earlier." Then we would discuss the core reason that caused him or her to have to stay after class in the first place.

A big part of EQ is getting to the core of the problem. After discussing the *why* with them ("Why did this become a problem in the first place?") then we could discuss the *what* and the *how* ("What are the options we have to handle this problem?" "How are we going to handle it?").

## SUPER CHICKENS

Recently I was talking to a friend of mine, a college coach in Nevada. He said he was struggling to figure his team out. They had a ton of talent from their valley but were "consistently inconsistent," as he put it. One game they would play extremely well and the next it was like they had never played together.

"I recruited the top athletes in our valley," he told me. "They are all gifted scorers but I can't get them to stop being selfish. Everyone wants the ball all the time." And that's when I told him about *super chickens*.

William Muir, a professor at the University of Purdue, wanted to determine what could make groups more productive. He decided on an experiment that involved chickens. William first found a flock of chickens that were productive. Some of the chickens only produced one egg per day and some produced more. He left them alone for six generations and didn't interfere with them in any way. As he said it, he just "let chickens do what chickens do."

Next, he created a separate flock made up of "super chickens" and only kept the birds that produced the most eggs. He continued this process so that only the more productive chickens would be together.

After six generations of the experiment, he compared the amount of eggs that the two flocks had laid. What he found was rather amazing: Not only did the average group of chickens produce more, but they were also doing amazingly well. They were all plump, fully feathered, and very healthy. As for the super chicken flock, not only did they produce less, but all but three were still alive. The rest had pecked each other to death.

The brilliant concept behind this study is that we think we need to be the "best of the best" to succeed. We teach ourselves that we can only achieve our goal by outproducing others...and by keeping those

2.

OK

thoughts in our head, we teach ourselves to "peck" each other to death.

What we need is a different approach. We need to build social capital, and social capital is another word for *trust*. Just like money, social capital compounds. We need to have time to get to know one another for our relationships to grow. Time is the only thing that compounds, even as you spend it. If you cannot get the "super chickens" on your team to buy into this concept, chances are your program is going to be chicken soup.

## 12 ROCKS OF COACHING TO BUILD A TEAM & PROGRAM

The following is excerpted from "12 Rocks of Coaching to Build a Team and Program" by Jack Bennett, former head coach at UW-Stevens Point, who led his team to back-to-back NCAA DIII national championships.

1. **Be Who You Are.** You can study the game, view instructional videos, and trust mentors. However, in the end you must be true to yourself. Coach *what you know and like.*

2. **Simplify the Game.** The greatest teachers are the people who can explain and break down complicated concepts into lessons that their pupils can understand. Coaching is

teaching. If you're confused and tentative, you can bet your players will be as well.

3. **The Game is Over-Coached and Under-Taught.** This ties into #2. Too many youth coaches try to put in systems and strategies that might win at that level but shortchange the really important skills kids need for future success. Players and teams must have a *vision* of what they can be down the road, not just in the now and present.

4. **Develop a Philosophy.** What is it you want your teams and individuals to be known for? How can a player know what's important if they don't know what you, as a coach, truly believe in?

5. **"Be Firm in Principle but Flexible in Approach."** Many years ago, a football coach stated that you must be a purist to some values, beliefs, and ways to teach and play the game. However, you must be pragmatic and smart enough to change certain things that are more attuned to your talent, times, and methods that will give your team the best chance for success.

6. **Be Tough and Compassionate.** The best people usually make the best coaches. Too

many coaches try to be dictators—a "my way or the highway" mentality. Others try to be buddies with their players. You must balance these two characteristics. The best know when mental toughness is demanded and understand when empathy and kindness are crucial. Being a coach is about personal relationships and trust.

7. **Define the Things you will not Compromise on.** What are your non-negotiables that are sacred to your program and execution? Share a few things your players know are not going to be tolerated if violated.

8. **Quality or Quantity—What is it You Want Your Program and Team to Stand for?** Fans, the media, and sometimes parents are into numbers: how many wins, how many minutes, how many points. If you do things honestly, ethically, and the right way (with *quality*), the numbers (*quantity*) will take care of themselves.

9. **Come to Terms with Winning and Losing.** Easier said than done. You must try to learn and be grateful for the wins and losses. Al McGuire said, "The greatest

emotion in sport is winning and the second greatest is losing." Of course success is more fun, but the ability to persevere and bounce back from disappointment separates genuine winners from losers.

Being humbled can lead to future success if we learn the right lessons. Winning and being puffed up with false pride can lead to future defeat if we can't stay grounded and hungry.

*"You can't let victory go to your head and you can't allow defeat to go to your heart."*

— *Unknown*

10. **Serve One Another.** Basketball is a team game. You must lean on one another and make your teammates better. If personal success is most important, compete in swimming, wrestling, or track and field, as team sports demand sacrifice and servanthood.

11. **GIYBALWI.** Give It Your Best And Live With It! My team and I used this acronym each and every time we took the court. If we prepared, practiced, and played to our full potential, we could live with whatever happened. If we cut corners or took

shortcuts, then we had problems and had to do some "attitude adjustments."

12. **Have a Life Outside of Basketball.** Whether it's faith, family, or hobbies, nurture the things that will permit you to keep the "fire in your belly" and the passion needed to be good at your sport.

13. **Courage and Wisdom.** Have the courage to stand by your convictions when others are criticizing and second-guessing, and the wisdom to know when someone else has a better idea and admit you were wrong. John Wooden said it best: *"It's not who is right, but what is right."*

Jack's "12 Rocks" is full of emotionally intelligent qualities. I highly recommend revisiting these qualities often and implementing them into your program and life.

## TALKING POINTS

*Q: Why is EQ an important leadership trait?*

*Q: Think of your own "rocks" that you would like to incorporate into your own program. What would they be?*

- It is important to understand one another then assume and it is important to make everyone feel as though there in as safe environment.

- I would like to have family place, my rules, good relationships, putting things important first.

# CHAPTER 9

*Recruiting the Best Players*

My grandfather told me once that you can make more friends in two months by being interested in them than you can in two years by trying to get them to be interested in you. The same goes for recruiting players. Show them that you're interested in them outside of their sports and they will be interested in your program.

If you want to gain an edge on recruiting, you must understand people. Typically there are three ways in which people process information. If you are oblivious to which way a person wants the information, you might lose their attention or become annoying to them. Listening to the way that they talk can give you valuable insights on how to proceed.

**Visual.** They want a picture of their future with your program. You can use phrases like "Let me show you what we have done for past players" or "Here is the big picture of what we want you to be a part of." They will enjoy seeing the campus and all of the amenities that come with the college experience. When a player can visually see themselves playing for your program, they will start to connect emotionally with it.

**Auditory.** A potential future team member might use phrases like "I hear you," "Sounds like…," and "Tell me more." They are not as concerned typically with visual information (graphs, booklets, etc.); they just want the information told to them, so you will need to learn to paint the picture of your program with the right words.

**Kinesthetic.** This person is much more deliberate in their speech. They are slow to answer and need time to process the information you are telling them. They will use phrases like "I need to get my mind around this" or "I'm evaluating all my options." Be sure to take your time and do not bombard them with more information. They do not want to feel pressured into making a decision because they may have anxiety about making the wrong decision. The more patient you can be, the more available you are to answer questions when they arise, the more likely they are to commit to your program.

## THE HARD AND SOFT SKILLS OF RECRUITING

Knowledge of EQ and the hard and soft skills of recruiting will change the way coaches recruit. Some coaches want to show how much they win, how nice their facilities are, or how many students attend the games. These are factors that certainly play into a student making a decision on where to attend school. They are called "hard skill" selling points.

However, paying all the attention to the hard skills often makes them forget the "soft skill" side. Coaches don't take time to understand a recruit's family life, who they hang out with, where they came from, how they were raised, their hobbies, or what they want to accomplish in life after sports. Being interested in your player's life will give you insight into their personality and why they may react or handle pressure situations differently.

Think about the best and worst teams you have ever coached or played on. Why did some win and others fail? Was it lack of skill, desire, work ethic, bad attitudes, or bad coaching/teaching? Why do some teams always find a way to win even when they have less skilled players?

They had leaders that have a higher EQ than those that didn't. To put it plainly, the players and coaches respected each other and they loved competing to attain a shared goal. They didn't let petty things get in the way of their progress and they genuinely cared about one another. Recruiting players with higher EQ will take your program to new heights.

During my senior year of high school, I had worked hard over the summer to keep the starting role for the upcoming season. We had a small rotation and our starting five was our most productive. We had young role players and we needed more scoring when our top two scorers came out.

Early in the season my coach approached me during practice and asked me if I would be willing to sacrifice my starting spot and come off the bench. You can imagine my disappointment when I first heard this. He explained that this was in no way a demotion, but rather we just needed more scoring from the bench.

Every coach knows that the most important thing in a team sport is not whether you start the game, but that you are trusted to be out there at the end. Unfortunately, most players do not understand this. So before I let my disappointment get the better of me, I stepped back and realized that I was going to have a chance to be a bigger part of the offense. I was still going to be on the floor just as much (if not more) and be able to contribute in a better way.

Of course, the selfish side of me still didn't like the fact that I was asked to come off the bench. In my head I felt like I deserved to be a starter because of all of the hard work I had put in over the last few years, but I was willing to do whatever it took to win. I knew I was not above the team and accepted my new role. I was willing to make that sacrifice if my coach thought it was best for the team and I didn't let my emotions get the best of me.

After a few games I was returned to the starting lineup. However, I'm sure that if I had a bad attitude about coming off the bench, I most certainly would not have been asked to start again. Attitude really is everything and fortunately I didn't let it affect me in a negative way.

## STOP NEGATIVE RECRUITING

Stop trying to overcome objections by negative recruiting. I don't know how you feel, but I absolutely *hate* election time! I cannot stand the negative campaigning that happens between the two parties. For months I am bombarded with commercial after commercial, each one telling me how bad the other candidate is. And unfortunately, much like a politician, some coaches want to point out the flaws that other programs have.

My coach said it best when people criticize others. He said, "Sometimes you run across people who go into a city and they put in the time and effort to build the tallest building. Then there are others who go into the same city and cut yours down so that theirs can look bigger." Focus on the vision of your program and making it bigger and better and spend less time on what others are doing.

If you are curious as to why potential new team members might be considering another school, it's okay to ask why. What do they have that we don't? You might find out that they have more objections about coming to your program than you think. Personally, I always want to know about my weaknesses as much as I want to know about my strengths.

Would you rather know about these objections before or after you spend a lot of time recruiting them? More than likely, they have already thought about those objections. If there is a continuing pattern of recruits bringing up the same objections, then you will know where to start to fix your recruiting deficiency.

## DO YOU KNOW YOUR RECRUIT?

If you were asked to write a paragraph about your recruit outside of his or her skill set, could you do it?

If you don't get to know about your recruit's family life, school life, and social life, then you don't know anything about them. You cannot relate to someone you know nothing about!

Here is a small list of questions and ideas for you to cover when recruiting an athlete.

1. **Ask your recruit to tell you about his or her workout program.** Request a list of places they play their sport or gyms where they work out. Ask them to describe in detail their off-season workout program. If they do not have a steady workout routine or do not show they can name the best places to get in a

pick-up game, chances are they don't work that hard in the off-season.

2. **Call the principal and ask for a list of teachers that your recruit has had recently.** Spend a day asking teachers' opinions of your recruit. While some opinions may differ, if you start to hear an underlying theme of positive or negative comments, you can assume that they are accurate. Also, do not be afraid to call coaches from opposing conferences and get their opinion of the player as well. Opposing coaches will typically be extremely honest with you, as they have no stock in your recruit.

3. **While on campus ask random students if they know your recruit.** I find that outgoing people have a wide variety of friends. If you are constantly running into students who know your recruit and have positive opinions about him or her, I believe they will have a good connection with your players as well.

4. **Ask teachers and students about the people your recruit spends the most time with.** I'm a firm believer in this because if you find out as much as you can about your recruits' friends, you will find out what kind of person your recruit is! I believe that 99% of

the time, you are who you hang out with. I also want to know if they have friends that are being recruited by other schools. If their friends are being recruited, they probably hang out with people that have a great work ethic as well.

5. **Ask them about their hobbies and goals after school.** I always want to see if I can connect with a person in any way possible. You should want to do the same with your recruit. Even if you cannot find a similar passion, a different coach or player is likely to have something in common with them.

For example, ask them about their work experience. Maybe reach out to a former employee and see what they say about your player. What they do for extra cash can be telling about their character. Ask them about the last movie they saw, the last book they read or the last concert they went to. Sometimes this can give you an insight on their sense of humor and a look into their social lives. Ask them how they feel about their current coach and the system they play in. If they are quick to criticize the coach or teammates, this might be a red flag—or maybe the coach is not a good person and the kid has it right. It will just require some more work on your side to figure out which is true.

## LEARN THE SKILL OF
## MIRRORING & MATCHING

The skill of mirror-matching is important for you to make your recruit feel comfortable. Have you ever thought about why you hang around the people that you do? It's probably because they are like you.

*Be aware of your communication style.* If the person or group you are with is laid back, match that style. If they are more energetic, become a little more animated. When you match their style, it makes them more comfortable and builds rapport.

I was attending a friend's college practice one day when I saw this skill ignored. They had a recruit watching from the stands with his high school coach and the practice had just ended. The assistant coach had an energetic and intense personality. The player, on the other hand, was relaxed and reserved. As soon as he walked up to the recruit, he slapped him on the back and squeezed his shoulder. He spoke at a fast pace and was extremely close to his face as he engaged with him. I immediately noticed that the athlete was uncomfortable with the coach breaking his "proximity bubble." He began to squirm in his seat and move back. The farther the recruit moved away, the closer the coach moved in.

It was two contrasting styles and I could tell the recruit was not enjoying his experience. Some people are okay with physical contact and some are not. Until you get to know a person, it is definitely better to refrain from anything other than a handshake. This particular coach was not attuned to his recruit's personality and it clearly made him uncomfortable.

Was this enough to make him not want to play for the program? I am guessing probably not. But in the world of recruiting, if a player has a better connection with a different assistant coach, it definitely could.

## LISTEN BEFORE YOU REACT

The emotional intelligence skill uses impulse control, emotional self-awareness, problem solving, and empathy to uncover a person's true "pain" or underlying problem. It allows you to listen and learn his or her story *before* you offer premature solutions.

Learn to listen first and speak second. A lot of times, the first problem a team member presents to you is not the real problem. We typically listen with the intent to reply rather than listen to absorb and analyze the information. Good problem solvers ask the questions that *get to the emotion* that is causing the problems.

## MANAGE YOUR RECRUITING EMOTIONS

So many times I see people want to close, close, close the deal. Who doesn't like getting something you really want? But managing your expectations when it comes to meeting with a potential recruit can be vital to whether or not the kid commits. Much like walking onto a used car lot, the last thing people want is for some guy to pressure you into making a quick decision in his favor. If you have ever felt duped before, you know that it's not a great feeling. The last thing anyone wants to feel is that they made a big mistake.

Too many coaches go into a recruiting meeting with the wrong intention: to close the player.

When you approach these meetings, do so with a different mindset: to find the truth and make sure the player is a good fit for *both* parties.

In any situation where you are selling something, the last thing you want to hear is "No." But far too many people are not comfortable with this word. In order to do your job and handle objections, you need to get comfortable with hearing no and lose the attachment to it.

In order to get to your ultimate goal, you need to ask the questions that make the most sense for the recruit. Your ultimate goal is to find the correct fit for your team and for the recruit. Sometimes after asking the right questions, maybe hearing a no is better than hearing a yes. When you lose the attachment to the outcome, you can focus more on the hidden objectives that might cause a recruit to be hesitant in joining your team. By asking the right types of questions, you can make them feel more comfortable and get much more honest answers.

## TALKING POINTS

*Q: What EQ qualities do you look for in recruits?*

*Q: Can you define three traits of great team players?*

- I don't think I'm old enough to look for a recruite yet but probably someone who is a leader and knows what they want also EQ'ed to.

- They are leader, they have empathy, They listen to the players on there team, and know when enough is enough.

# CHAPTER 10
*Building a Culture of EQ*

Culture is "the set of shared attitudes, values, goals, and practices that characterizes an institution or organization."[14] Building a culture of EQ in your program means choosing your players over your process. You have to get them to understand that *they* define the idea of culture by their attitude and their actions! Teams that promote a strong, emotionally intelligent culture typically have these common traits:

1. **They promote learning.** Emotionally intelligent sports programs include teaching life skills outside of their sport. They offer life skill training and treat it as an investment in their player's future so they can continue to be successful in their social and professional lives.

I knew a coach who made players attend a "dinner etiquette" class so that they don't embarrass themselves at dinner functions in front of important people. He also made first-year students attend a cooking class at least one time before the season started. As a way to practice their new life skill and get the guys together to bond, the players had to plan and

14 Merriam-Webster.

cook one team meal for everyone at the coach's house. Another coach I know makes his players help the managers do the laundry one time throughout the year.

Examples like this will promote and encourage players to be close with each other and more loyal to the program. (By the way, I highly encourage programs to steal this idea!) The more you show you care about their future, the more they will look back in the past with love and appreciation for you and the time they had in school.

Build a culture of EQ in your program: Create a learning environment. Find small articles on emotional intelligence and read them once a month. Share an experience in which you used an EQ technique to solve a problem that you had, and have each player do the same. Make sure to point out high EQ qualities or decisions that were made during practice or games. Using EQ language will help with this process. The best part is that once they see the positive effects that it has on the program, the more likely they will use it in their own life and teach it to their children or kids they may coach one day.

2. **They value collaboration.** This includes listening to insight from their peers, staff, managers, and coaches. Teamwork is a core value in teams that consistently perform well. I'm not necessarily talking about teamwork in

terms of the way to play during a game. I'm talking about teams that make sure each team member is getting the help he or she needs to be successful in life. Everyone plays a role in building a winning culture. It takes a "collaboration village" to achieve this.

Build a culture of EQ in your program: Get rid of selfish attitudes. "You get more by giving more" is a core value that teams with high EQ possess. It's easy to say, but difficult to do. I always tell players if you have knowledge or a skill that can help a person out, share it. If someone is new on the team, take them out and put a real effort into getting to know their story. I see a new player struggle all the time because they are not used to the demands of the college lifestyle. They may struggle with the difficulty of classes, new coaching or teammates personalities, the physicality and intensity of practices, or the overall stresses of being someplace new. In college homesickness is a very real thing and your experiences can help them grow faster, shorten their learning curve to fit in and get comfortable with the program.

If someone is in a slump, spend extra time to help him or her through it. Pay attention to body language and conversations you have with your teammates. It can give you a lot of information about what's going on in their life. Most of all, if something is bothering you, *share it with someone*. Keep in mind that when a player opens up to you, they're saying they trust you. You have to keep that trust by not making light of their story and listening with the intent to help.

How many of you would help your teammates out if you knew it could lead to them taking your playing time or starting spot? Would you still do it? I say only the very special teams do.

3. **They encourage philanthropy by servant leadership.** Servant leadership is the act of giving or doing for someone without expecting anything in return. In other words, it has little to do with *what* you do for others and more to do with your *attitude toward others*. It's leading with your heart.

Build a culture of EQ in your program: Recognize and be grateful. In order for you to be where you are today, you had to have received help from someone along the way. No one can achieve success alone! Praise and recognition are the easiest, most inexpensive things you can give to someone— yet the knowledge and advice that is passed along is priceless.

When was the last time someone sent you a hand-written thank-you note? When was the last time you truly felt appreciated for your efforts? When someone does a good job, make sure you point it out. If they consistently go above and beyond and are never recognized for it, they will surely not do it anymore. *Do not* take the efforts of others for granted!

Search out the people who help run your program and thank them for their work: administrators, faculty, the janitor, the catering personnel, and most importantly the people who come to your games. There is one thing that I have learned about gratitude: that no one ever complains about being over-appreciated.

Teams and programs that give back to the community and to each other promote social responsibility. They see that by giving to each other they gain more than just stats or wins in a season. They learn the value of kindness, generosity and gratitude, which will result in success for the rest of their life. Contrary to popular belief, leadership is not about the number of people you lead, but rather the number of people who are willing to follow you when it counts the most. We will discuss leadership in more detail later in the book.

## HOW TO DEVELOP EQ WITHIN YOUR SPORTS PROGRAM

1.  **Schedule downtime.** Since self-awareness is a key foundation for building and improving emotional intelligence skills, it helps a player gain insight as to how they approach practice and team functions. It enlightens your players on how their attitude, behavior, and actions

affect themselves inside and outside of your program.

Players who tend to have low EQ are not self-aware, do not change, and they often make the same mistakes that result in negative outcomes. He or she will often blame others for their failures because they cannot recognize that their actions are the cause of the problems. Since you cannot change what you are not aware of, the more time you give your players to learn about themselves, the better they will be. This section of the program will give an athlete the foundation to become aware.

2. **Create technology-free zones.** People, especially young adults, are not good at multitasking. When it comes time to practice, a player loses the ability to focus for extended periods of time. Set aside time for students to completely disconnect from their devices. This includes the coaching staff. My recommendation is that technology should never be allowed in an area where there is a team function—including locker rooms, team dinners, and charity events with the public. I often see athletes sitting in the locker room before games or directly after practice looking at their phones, ignoring each other. The worst place that this happens is at team

functions where they ignore the public. It sends a message that they are not as important as your phone.

Our brain is created to process and interpret both new and old information. It is meant to be challenged and evolve. You cannot change how you think and feel without changing your brain. Understanding how your brain works helps you to be more successful. Learn to use your real brain, not the iPhone brain.

3. **Delay gratification.** You may have heard me mention this term earlier in the book. Delayed gratification is the ability to wait before achieving a reward. The most famous study done by a researcher was called the "marshmallow test" or the Stanford study. A group or four-year-olds were given a choice. A single marshmallow would be left in a room with the child and the instructor told them that he was going to run an errand and he would be gone for twenty minutes. He said that they could eat the marshmallow as soon as he left the room—but if they didn't eat the marshmallow before he came back, they would get two marshmallows.

The kids who participated in this study were followed into their professional careers and it was noted that the students who were able to delay gratification and not eat the marshmallow were much more successful in their social and professional lives.

An athlete who delays gratification will get their work done before anything else. They understand that procrastinating will hinder the team's growth. He or she doesn't take shortcuts and cheat to attain their goals. They make good decisions when they are out with their friends and get back home without incident. Temptation is not easily given into because they have personal and professional goals and make decisions based on attaining those goals.

*Ask yourself:* Are you willing to delay gratification for a chance to win a conference, state, or national championship? I believe that the most successful people do!

## APPLYING EQ VIA COMMUNICATION

When I meet a new coach for the first time, I often ask if there is something that they would like me to focus on when I do my program. Ninety-nine out of a hundred times they want me to teach their players how to communicate better. You would think with the advances in our communication technology that it should be easy to communicate. However, that is clearly not the case. In fact, it is probably one of the reasons that we actually do not communicate face to face very well. When it comes to communication, one of the hardest things to do is to have the *entire* conversation.

Recently I got to see author and speaker JP Pawliw-Fry talk at a conference in Wisconsin. He is the author of *Performing Under Pressure: Doing Your Best When It Matters Most*. During his presentation he stated that people typically only have 92% of the conversation when it comes to addressing conflict. The last 8% of the conversation is ignored because that's when criticism takes place; it's also the time when emotions are the strongest. We often get anxious and end up cutting the conversation short because we don't want to hurt the other person's feelings or we fear being attacked in return.

In order for the final 8% of the conversation to occur, certain things need to happen. I call this having "communication diplomacy."

Communication diplomacy happens when both people realize that there is a "gap" between the two sides of communication. It's called the "understanding gap." It's the gap that stops you from seeing or listening to the other person's point of view. Bridging this gap is crucial in order to have effective communication.

The understanding gap can be broken down into two parts: *intent* and *impact*. Think about the last time you offered someone advice and they took it the wrong way. How did you feel? Chances are you might have felt like they didn't appreciate that your *intent* was to help them. Maybe you felt unappreciated and became frustrated. But to the other person, the only thing they could see was how your advice made them feel (maybe judged or criticized)—they only felt the *impact* that it had on them and not your *intent*.

Now let's look at it from the other side. Think about the last time someone offered you advice you didn't ask for or perhaps it was more critical than you wanted. How did it impact your feelings? Did you get defensive or angry?

Since we feel before we think, you probably only felt the impact that the criticism had on you. You didn't stop to look at their intent, which was that they were probably only trying to help you. Understanding intent and impact will start the foundation to building a bridge over the communication gap.[15]

## THE "WHAT'S UP?" METHOD

When it comes to bridging the communication gap, that "gap" can sometimes feel more like a communication canyon. I think we have all been in situations when no matter what someone said, you could not see their point of view—or vice versa. A main key in raising your EQ is listening effectively, analyzing emotions, and reacting accordingly when speaking with others.

---

[15] Pawliw-Fry, JP. "Emotional Intelligence." Keynote speech, Green Bay, WI, 2014.

1. **Realize that the intent of most people when they offer advice is to help you out.** Your defenses will be down and your mind will be able to listen to and comprehend the information given to you. In most circumstances, you have no control over how the information is given to you, but you do have control over how it is received.

Someone's meaning when giving you advice is not always clear. Unfortunately, due to different communication styles, a person's well-meaning advice may come across as critical and rude. You have to be prepared to navigate those rough waters with a different outlook going into the conversation.

2. **"What's up?"** You may not realize that you have lost control of your emotions before it's too late. How do we not let the emotion of the moment get to you? I call this recognizing a "what's up" moment. As soon as a strong emotion hits your gut, rather than react, pause for a moment and think, "What's up?"

3. **Ask yourself what just caused you to have that reaction.** Pausing, even if it's for a moment, will be key to finding out what caused your "what's up?" moment. Then take

time to label the emotion. Try to figure out the exact emotion you are feeling. I found that guarding against a gut reaction emotional response will give you the ability to solve that problem and think of a better way to respond it.

4. **React responsibly.** Keep EQ in your mind at all times. When you react, ask yourself, "Do I need to respond right now or can it wait until I get my emotions in check?" "Is this an emotionally intelligent response?" An even better question I ask myself when I get stressed is "Will this bother me a year from now?" If the answer is no, you can easily move on. If it is yes, find a way to have the difficult conversation in the correct setting.

## CREATING YOUR OWN TEAM LANGUAGE

There was a study done as to why some people don't save money for their retirement. It was noted that people in general don't imagine what they would be doing if they were retired—and since they can't imagine it, they have no feeling or connection to it. People have a tendency to only be focused on their current condition, which causes them to live their life in a day-to-day fashion, never thinking about the future.[16]

Later in the experiment, the group was asked to draw a picture of what they thought they would be doing when they were retired. This technique forced them to imagine what their life would be like in the future. By them first drawing and then looking at the picture, it added a "realness" to their future retirement. They were asked to imagine the feeling they would have after attaining their goal in retirement.

A few months after the experiment was complete, three-quarters of participants reported that they were now saving for their retirement. The reason? They noted they had never been forced to think about the future before and it led to a lack of preparation.

The same can be accomplished in terms of preparing an athlete mentally to find a way to forge a common goal of winning championships.

Creating a team allegiance and its purpose is to help the athlete create a tribe mentality with their team—whether it's performing a welcome ceremony when a new member joins the team, or requiring current team members to make the new athlete a welcome gift. Keeping communication up among members of the team is critical to success whether

---

[16] Malito, Alessandra. "This is Why Most People Don't Save Money for Retirement." MarketWatch. October 22, 2016. Accessed January 26, 2018.
https://www.marketwatch.com/story/this-is-why-most-people-dont-save-money-for-retirement-2016-10-05.

you're a player or a coach; this important concept applies to all.

## WORKING WITH DIFFERENT PERSONALITIES

When applying good EQ techniques to team communication, learning how to work with different team members' personalities is the key. Sometimes, it's not clear why others think or act the way they do, but it's important to look deeply at the key causes behind their actions in order to better understand them and learn how to react.

For example, let's look at Jameis Winston. He was a college student playing football for Florida State University. He is currently the quarterback for the Tampa Bay Buccaneers. In early 2014 he was cited for allegedly stealing crab legs from a store. Why would a kid who is going to be making millions of dollars a year in the NFL steal?

While we don't know if Jameis actually intended to steal the crab legs, we do know that he took them without paying for them. We know that Winston made a decision to do something that had potential *severe* negative publicity and *severe* team ethical conduct code violations. He chose to do something bad, even when he knew there could be dire consequences for his actions. Yet, he still let his impulse control issues get the best of him. Earlier in his career he was accused of sexual assault, which almost wrecked his life. Does this sound like the actions of someone concerned about protecting his public image and the image of his team? Nope.

People under normal circumstances do not put themselves into a position where they can be accused of stealing—especially when they are in the public spotlight like he was.

Sometimes there are such deep issues that it doesn't matter what you tell a kid. They are never going to be able to grow or change because of those underlying issues that cause them to make bad decisions. Most coaches and the media might just write them off as a "bad kid" and kick them off the team.

But if you can get to the core of their problem and help them, you will have a family member for life. This is not to say that he or she deserves unlimited chances, but when people choose an action that could have bad consequences over their sports family, they have an underlying issue. I believe it's our responsibility to try to help that person find out what it is.

The same thing applies to a team's "personality." Why do some teams always start slow and then always come back and win in the second half of games? Why do some teams win most of the game, but fail to finish and lose? It's personality characteristics. EQ translates over to this as well. It could be nerves, culture, coaching style…any number of reasons. If you understand personalities and people, you can recognize, diagnose, and solve these issues when they arise.

# TALKING POINTS

*Q: What steps will you take to build a culture of EQ in your program?*

*Q: Can you give five tips for building an emotionally intelligent team?*

- I will try to understand people better and focus on the intent of advice instead of the impact.

- communication, team bonding, rules, know your players comforts, and stay up to date with them.

# CHAPTER 11
*Final Points*

Emotional intelligence is the key to a successful sports season and an unbeatable, close-knit team. It is my hope that during the process of this book, you have learned the basic tenets of emotional intelligence and how developing these skillsets can impact your life and your role on a sports team for the better.

Below are a few final points to keep in mind during your continued journey to improved EQ.

1. **Be likable.** Being likable is a major part of having a high EQ. What is the reason you like someone? How can you tell if someone really likes you? Can you explain it? Sometimes it's easy—maybe they have a great sense of humor. Maybe you have a strong connection based on a shared experience or sometimes it's just a gut feeling.

2. **Be approachable.** If you want to become more likable, always be aware of your body language. If your arms are crossed, you're hunched over and aren't making eye contact, you're putting out the universal sign for "DO NOT BOTHER ME!"

On the contrary, if you have a smile, are making eye contact, and your palms are facing up, it means that you are willing to be engaged. Looking people in the eyes can tell much about how you are feeling. In fact, it's really hard to hide because the eyes are the gateway to a person's "feeling" soul.

My friend Matt uses the term "bright eyes" to classify someone who is approachable and friendly. These are the people who are authentic. They take time to be interested in other people's lives and are not afraid to show it. Try to apply the "bright eyes" mentality to your daily life to improve your EQ and likability.

3. **Be genuine.** This is a tough thing to do for some people, especially when we live in a society that makes it easy to criticize one another. Nevertheless, it's so important for you to be yourself. Working with EQ is great because it will help you become the type of person that will make it easier for you to do this. Are you being your sincere self or are you showing up as someone else?

4. **Show empathy.** The fastest way to become likable is to show that you're interested in helping them—not because of what they can do for you, but because you just want to help.

Business doesn't always work like this. You may help someone because you know that if you do, they might help you back by becoming a client—and this is 100% okay.

The problem that arises is when you *expect* something in return. If you only care about the business side, you'll ultimately lose because the client will see that you have no interest in getting to know them better. They will see that money or another selfish purpose was your ultimate goal. Are you a giver or a taker? Who have you helped recently and why did you do it?

## THE MASTERY GAP

It's important to understand that when you first learn a new skill, you are probably going to fail at it. It takes time for your brain to process the information in your neural pathways because your brain is wired to use your old techniques. The time in between you breaking an old skill or habit and creating a new one is called the "mastery gap." It's the time that you feel the most uncomfortable while learning your new skill; during this time, you can quickly become frustrated—especially if you are not getting the desired results quick enough.

If you cannot manage these emotions, you will be likely to return to what you feel the most comfortable with, even if you know it is inferior to the new way. Remember, change is scary for individuals; it takes time to process the information and even more time to see the desired results.

Improving your EQ will take time, dedication, hard work, and conscious effort. However, over time you will undoubtedly notice a difference in the quality of your relationships, and bond between the other members of your sports team, better communication, and improved teamwork.

While I am trying to help players and coaches create team chemistry by using EQ for sports, more importantly, I am trying to give you skills for navigating the tricky waters of *life*.

Lastly, I want to end at the beginning. My hope is that when times are tough, you will think about Francis and the canoe. My ultimate goal is to help everyone who reads this book to use what they learned to "leave the canoe" and never be afraid to "get back in the water" for someone else—even if you barely know them. If we do that, we're winners…no matter the score of a game. And that, my friends, is the *real magic*!

*"Success is what happens after you have survived all your mistakes."*

*– Anora Lee*

# TEAM EXERCISES

*"When you are done learning, you are done!"*

*– John Wooden*

## JOHN WOODEN'S "CHEMISTRY PYRAMID"

When I work with a team, the first thing I want them to understand is team chemistry. If you ask five different coaches their definition of chemistry, you will probably get five different answers. That's why it's important for *your* team to define team chemistry. It will give your players a sense of ownership and make it much easier to hold each other accountable.

First, have *your team* define team chemistry in their own words. What words would they use ("togetherness," "dedication," "hard work") to describe team chemistry? Create a list of those words.

Once a list of ten to twenty words are compiled, draw a "John Wooden" pyramid, as shown below.

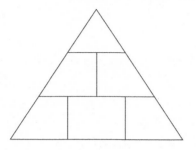

Pick six words off of the list that your team feels best represents the team's idea of what chemistry means.

Together, place the words inside the pyramid and explain why they are choosing the words. Where they choose to put the words inside the pyramid should hold value as well: More important words go at the top; words that go at the bottom of the pyramid represent the foundation of the team's beliefs—without a solid foundation, they feel their chemistry pyramid would crumble.

Have someone from the team put this on a big poster board and hang it up in the locker room for all to see.

## THE STRONGEST LINK

I am sure you have heard the saying, "You are only as strong as your weakest link."

I believe that is wrong.

Think about this: You are only as good as your *strongest* link. Your strongest link is someone that helps create a team bond so strong that it's unbreakable, impenetrable. It's the link that refuses to allow the other links to fail.

Let's put this to a test. Get a bunch of carabiners and give each teammate and coach one to decorate. You could have a word or phrase on it or maybe a quote that motivates you. Be creative!

Instruct your team members to keep it with them at all times during the day. Clip it to their backpack or duffle bag so it doesn't get forgotten or lost. If a player forgets or loses his carabiner, the team must create a penalty for the mistake!

At the beginning of every practice, players must give their carabiner to the coach and "link" them to the head coach's carabiner for the duration of practice. After practice, they can be given back to the player. I believe it's a great visual to go with a new concept!

# APPENDIX A

*Jack Bennett Interview*

*Jack Bennett is considered one of the greatest basketball coaches in Wisconsin with a career record of 480-175. After taking over at the University of Wisconsin Stevens Point, he amassed a record of 200-56, 5 WIAC post-season titles and 5 trips to the NCAA Division III post-season where he won back to back NCAA titles in and was until recently the highest winning coach in UWSP history. I was fortunate enough to be able to talk to Jack about his philosophy on coaching and team chemistry.*

**Me:** Tell me about your philosophy and thought process when you coached.

**Jack:** We live in a society that everything is based on numbers. And I'm not telling you that numbers are not important—that's why we keep the schedule and pay attention to the standings—BUT again, you are asking about the best teams. Well, we had a standard that we had to play to. I said are we going to accept in victory what we wouldn't accept in defeat? It's an old statement, but there are going to be times that we are going to get beat, but inside I know that we probably played as well as we could.

**Me:** Like Marquette? (UWSP had just come off of their first title under Jack and were picked to play in an exhibition game against Marquette the following season.)

**Jack:** Yes, for sure. I knew we were going to be a good team after that game. There was a situation where we said we did things right, we didn't beat ourselves, we just got beat by a more talented group. And there are times when you beat someone and didn't play as hard, you were able to get by because we had better individual talent. I was always trying to think ahead: Would this be good enough to beat Whitewater in the WIAC or would this be good enough to beat Texas Trinity? I think sometimes too many fans and young coaches get lost in the numbers. "Well, we just won five in a row." Sure, but each game you are playing more selfishly, you just beat them because you were better. I just wanted to know: Is this good enough to beat the best?

**Me:** Who was the best leader you ever had in the locker room?

**Jack:** "The last three to four years I coached it was Nick (Bennett) and (Jason) Kalsow. And they were tough sometimes. When they practiced they *hated* to get beat. There were sometimes I would tell the gold squad, our third squad, "You try to beat that first team," because I wanted to see how they would react. But they would just hate to lose. But off the court they would hang out a lot. Sure, they may have had their differences. All teams do, but that didn't stop them from all from having the same goal. I think the word "chemistry" is a vague term and is quite often overused. John Wooden said it best: "I don't like all of my players equally, and they don't have to like each other equally. But they had better love each other equally."

I think that there are a select few programs that actually understand that term. Not many coaches really understand what chemistry is. Heck, I don't even know if *I* truly understand that term…chemistry.

**Me:** But I think you do, Coach. If you go through the principles of my book, it has this stuff in it. It's just that you didn't call it emotional intelligence. The guys that actually do buy into it are the ones who truly get it. I am just trying to put a name to chemistry. I look at emotional intelligence and chemistry like baking a cake. I know the ingredients, but if I gave you a pound of flour, a pound of salt, a pound of sugar, a dozen eggs, a tub of butter, a bottle of vanilla extract and a can of baking powder, you could actually bake a cake. If you have no training and have never been taught how much of each ingredient to put in to make a good cake, it's probably going to not be very good at first. It's going to take time, dedication, and hard work to keep trying new recipes and not give up. Everyone is different and we are complicated beings. Chemistry is exactly the same—it's trial and error but mostly it's on the players. You, as a coach, are just supplying the ingredients.

**Jack:** Yes, that's it. You just said it: Everyone is different. You are going have to write your book your way. There will be things that you use that are going to be different from other writers and it's the same with coaches.

Sure, you can mimic other coaches but you cannot *be* other coaches. I listened to Bobby Knight, but I never wanted to be Bobby Knight. I knew I had to take the things I like and make them my own. I knew I had to be myself. I had to be genuine.

You asked what the secret was—the greatest team I ever coached—there was that *trust*. It wasn't like the players had their agenda and the coaching staff had their agenda, they would say we are all on the same page. They may have a difference of opinion on how we are doing it once in a while, but we are all heading in the same direction.

# APPENDIX B

*Interview with John Cook*

*Nebraska Cornhuskers volleyball team head coach John G. Cook is in his 19th season. In 2000, 2006, 2015, and 2017 he led the Huskers to four national championships, and he is a two-time winner of the AVCA National Coach of the Year award. As of 2018, Cook's record at Nebraska is 531–69. Cook has further proven his fabulous track record as previous head coach of the Wisconsin Badgers, where he managed a 161–73 record over seven seasons.*

**Me:** What does your program value most at Nebraska?

**John:** Two things: hard work and Nebraska volleyball. So, not putting yourself before Nebraska volleyball. This is about Nebraska volleyball, the team, the program, and making sure they are all in on that. It's not about them. That's one of the tings we fight the most. They (the players) are worried about their stats or their play and I want them to know it's about the team. In fact, if I see an interview with the word "I" in it, I highlight it and make sure to remind them that it's not about you, its about "us" and "we." It's about Nebraska volleyball.

**Me:** You've had teams that have won national titles but when we talked earlier about team chemistry, you said that there is one particular team that stands out—a team that didn't win a championship. Can you tell me about that team?

**John:** I was having nightmares before the season. I thought this could be one of the worst teams in Nebraska history. And so what happened was Jordon. Jordon was a very highly—she was a "McDonalds all American" if you want to call it that. Her freshman year was 2005 and we played Washington in the National Championship match and she had 1 kill in 25 attempts. So her first big stage moment...she played awful. In 2006 she had a much better year and we won the National Championship and in 2007 she did really well. But she showed no leadership. She didn't care about anything else except playing and getting as good as she can get and go pro.

What happened was I'm away recruiting and Jordan calls me. Some people would say that my 2007 team was the most talented in the history of college volleyball. We had two national players of the year on that team...we had the best setter I have ever had, it was just loaded. We graduated four all Americans off of that team and they way underperformed. We lost in the regional finals that year. But in the beginning of the year, there was no one that could touch us. I think they just got bored. We had a player after the season who does an interview with our school newspaper and she just unloaded on our team. Unloaded on how much no one appreciated her, no one liked her—this full-page article came out in the school newspaper. So Jordon sees it and calls me in Omaha and says, "Coach, you have to get down here right now." I asked her what's going on and she asked me if I had seen the article. Basically in the article she just vented and trashed everyone on her way out because they didn't win it last year.

So I get in my car and drive back and they are all sitting in our ready room. They tell me all of this and Jordan is irate. I look in and Jordan is running the show and I have never seen this from her before. She's like, "We are going to show the world and we are going to prove her wrong." And she's like pointing and doing the talk.

I'm like, "Where is this coming from?"

If I'm not mistaken, you talked about this in your book. You said there are moments that kind of create leadership opportunities."

**Me:** Yes, yes exactly.

**John:** This was her: "I'm going to put this team on my back moment and we are going to prove everybody wrong." So that's where it started.

Then our setter sprains her ankle...and now we have to use our back up setter. She's only our setter for like a week as we are trying to prepare for opening the season against Stanford and USC who are ranked two and three in the country.

So anyway, we get our setter back and we go and beat both Stanford and USC 3-0 in the first weekend and I'm like, "What the hell just happened?" I can't even believe it. And this team because of what Jordon, as a leader... They just responded so much through all of that experience and knowing that we might not even have a setter...that they all just had to pick up the slack because they knew that we all have to do this or we don't even have a chance. It was amazing to see these girls come together.

We exceeded far more that what I thought we would do and we get to the regional finals—this is against Washington and to show you how much emotional intelligence they had and how much grit they had...we lost both middle blockers to injury. So we are down two setting blockers and we have two walk-on middles playing in this match.

Anyway, we get down 2-0 against Washington who is ranked number one in the country at Washington. We come back to win games three and four because Jordon is just taking over the match. We go down 9-3 in the fifth at Washington—I mean, it's over. I call my last time out and I don't remember what I said but we came back and won and Jordon just took over.

**Me:** What happened?

**John:** There were two interesting things that happened: One is Jordan became a leader in February and took that team. The other thing was the dynamic—and this is where I would love to show you this video on somebody's "why." You know, what motivates them or what forces them to have that grit and dig down deep.

Jordon's mom had breast cancer—so that spring when this happened and her mom was diagnosed, her mom was going though chemo and the night before we beat Michigan in Seattle, her mom was so sick and flew out to Seattle but she couldn't make it for the Washington match. I really believe Jordon said to herself, "I'm not letting my mom miss my last match." And if you watch the comeback, Jordon was involved in every point—killing it, blocking it, digging it, serving it. It's just…it was like almost a miracle to watch this thing, and I think Jordon's "why" was really strong. She knew her mom was sitting in the hotel…and if we won this match we get to come back to Omaha and play the final four at home. That motivated those kids and they played out of their minds. I still think the Washington coach can't believe what happened. *I* still can't believe what happened. But anyway, we came back and played in the final four in Omaha and Jordon's mom was able to come back and watch her final match at home.

**Me:** Did you win your semi-final game?

**John:** No. So that was the match that we played Penn State and Penn State hadn't lost a set… Okay, we're not talking a match, they hadn't lost a set *all year*! This is like the UConn of women's volleyball. They had four future Olympians on that team and I'm watching them warm up and I'm like, "Holy… well at least we got here." There were 17,000 people there and these guys were like rock stars because everybody watched that match in Washington and that great comeback, they knew the story of Jordon's mom. I mean it was…it was like a movie.

It was the same thing: We go down 2-0 and we are just crushed the first two games, I meant the scores are like 12 and 13 points and we just get blown out of the gym. And then game three we start playing great. We crush Penn State 25-15 and then the next game we beat them 25-19 and we go onto the fifth and we are tied at 11-11 and the crowd in this unbelievable atmosphere and—I still have all the letters, I can go dig them up of people who said it was the greatest sporting event they have ever seen. Anyway, we ended up losing 13-15 in the fifth. But talk about a team that maxed out everything that they had.

**Me:** That's what I tell coaches. I'm careful to let them know that just because your team has high emotional intelligent players *doesn't* mean you are going to win a national championship. I mean, you have to have talent too. But what it does mean is that you are going to *maximize* that talent. And that could mean winning half of your conference games or winning more than what your skill level is supposed to win. It might even lead to the excitement of winning it all. But without it, you don't have a shot!

# TEAM-BUILDING
# EQ QUESTIONNAIRE

We invite you to use our Team-Building EQ Questionnaire to find the impact that Emotional Intelligence has on your team's performance:

| | | | | | | | |
|---|---|---|---|---|---|---|---|
| I have a good sense of why I have certain feelings most of the time. | 1 | 2 | 3 | 4 | 5 | 6 | 7 |
| I have good understanding of my own emotions. | 1 | 2 | 3 | 4 | 5 | 6 | 7 |
| I really understand what I feel. | 1 | 2 | 3 | 4 | 5 | 6 | 7 |
| I always know whether or not I am happy. | 1 | 2 | 3 | 4 | 5 | 6 | 7 |
| I always know my team members' emotion from their behavior. | 1 | 2 | 3 | 4 | 5 | 6 | 7 |
| I am a good observer of other's emotions. | 1 | 2 | 3 | 4 | 5 | 6 | 7 |
| I am sensitive to the feelings and emotions of others. | 1 | 2 | 3 | 4 | 5 | 6 | 7 |
| I have good understanding of the emotions of people around me | 1 | 2 | 3 | 4 | 5 | 6 | 7 |
| I always set goals for myself and then try my best to achieve the | 1 | 2 | 3 | 4 | 5 | 6 | 7 |
| I always tell myself that I am a competent person. | 1 | 2 | 3 | 4 | 5 | 6 | 7 |
| I am motivated to do a task without needing pressure from othe | 1 | 2 | 3 | 4 | 5 | 6 | 7 |
| I would always encourage myself to try my best. | 1 | 2 | 3 | 4 | 5 | 6 | 7 |
| I am able to control my temper and handle difficulties wisely. | 1 | 2 | 3 | 4 | 5 | 6 | 7 |
| I am quite capable of controlling my own emotions. | 1 | 2 | 3 | 4 | 5 | 6 | 7 |
| I can always calm down quickly when I am angry. | 1 | 2 | 3 | 4 | 5 | 6 | 7 |
| I have good control of my own emotions. | 1 | 2 | 3 | 4 | 5 | 6 | 7 |

## ABOUT THE AUTHOR

James David was a high school and college basketball player and later became a varsity head coach for five years and a varsity assistant for six years. He has worked with many teams including the Portland Trailblazers, the UCLA Bruins, and the University of Michigan, and earned awards including the King D Award, the Complete Player Award, and is a two-time Mr. Clutch Award recipient. He was a three-time California Interscholastic Federation Playoff participant, earning honors and honorable mentions. Today, he is a professional magician, speaker, and team builder. He currently lives in Stevens Point, Wisconsin with his wife Sarah and four boys Ben, Jayce, Tommy, and Preston.

Made in the USA
Las Vegas, NV
26 February 2021